Dating Rocks!

The 21 Smartest Moves Women Make for Love

STEVE NAKAMOTO

Java Books

Huntington Beach, California

"The world is not a playground; it's a schoolroom. Life is not a holiday, but an education. And the one eternal question for us all is how better we can love."

—Henry Drummond
Scottish philosopher (1851-1897)

Published by Java Books
17202 Corbina Lane, Suite 204
Huntington Beach, California 92649
E-mail: menarelikefish@mindspring.com
Phone/Fax: 714-846-0622

For More Information: www.DatingRocks.com

Books may be purchased for educational, business, or sales promotional use. For information, please write: Special Marketing, Java Books, 17202 Corbina Lane, Suite 204, Huntington Beach, CA 92649.

Cover Design by Pamela Terry, Opus 1 Design
Illustrations and Cartoons by Joe Kohl
Editing by Robin Quinn, Quinn's Word for Word
Author's Photo by Mike Colburn at www.emyimages.com

Publisher's Cataloging-in-Publication Data
Nakamoto, Steve.
    Dating rocks!: the 21 smartest moves women make for love/Steve
    Nakamoto. Huntington Beach, California, Java Books, 2006.
       p. cm.
    ISBN 0-9670893-4-4
       1. Relationships. 2. Self-help. 3. Psychology.
       I. Title.
HG567345.R454345   2006   2005908287
658.9   dc-21   CIP

03 02 01 00 ❦ 5 4 3 2 1

Printed in the United States of America

A Special Note to the Reader

*While it is common in today's culture for women to live
joyful, fulfilling lives without men, the reverse is rarely
true. French moralist, Jean de La Bruyere (1645-1696)
warned all men when he wrote, "A bachelor's life is a
fine breakfast, a flat lunch, and a miserable dinner."
So as a man, I am grateful for those women who still
seek love from us even though our actions sometimes
make relationships difficult.*

*Please note that the stories, examples, ideas, and word
choices in this book were generated and refined with the
help of my talented writing and editing contributors,
Shannon Gibbs, Dawn Borg, Toni Williams, and Robin
Quinn. Without their invaluable assistance, this book
would never have been completed at this quality.*

*And lastly, this book is dedicated to all the wonderful
men and women who have endured deep heartache and
disappointment, but still move forward in their love
lives knowing that the emotional gifts inside their hearts
were truly meant to be shared with someone special.*

*May this book provide you with the proper insights,
strategies, tools and, most of all, enlightened spirit.*

Disclaimer

This book is designed to provide information about the subject matter covered. It is sold with the understanding that the publisher and author are not engaged in rendering professional services of any kind. If expert assistance is required, the services of a competent professional should be sought first and foremost.

Every effort has been made to make this book as complete and accurate as possible. However, there may be mistakes, both in typography and in content. Therefore, this text should be used only as a general guide or a reference for exploring ideas, and not as the ultimate source of quality relationship, personal development, communication, or psychological information.

The stories set forth in this book, while based in part on fact, have been modified so as not to reveal the identity of any real person. Any resemblance between persons depicted in this book and real persons, living or dead, is strictly coincidental.

The purpose of this book is to enlighten, inspire, and entertain the reader. The author and publisher shall have neither liability nor responsibility to any persons or entity with respect to any loss or damage caused or alleged to be caused directly or indirectly by the information, ideas, and suggested assignments presented in this book.

If you do not wish to be bound by the statements above, you are entitled to return this book directly to the publisher, Java Books, for an immediate refund.

Contents

INTRODUCTION   7

1. DEAD-END ROMANCES   17
   Dating sucks when it goes nowhere

2. LOVE DECISIONS   29
   Dating rocks when you take charge of your love life

3. THE POWER SOURCE   39
   Dating rocks when you love yourself first

4. EXCESS BAGGAGE   51
   Dating sucks when the past weighs you down

5. BLIND SPOTS   61
   Dating sucks when you don't know your weaknesses

6. IRRESISTIBLE WOMEN   71
   Dating rocks when men find you desirable

7. LOSING CANDIDATES   83
   Dating sucks when you choose the wrong men

8. BAD ODDS   93
   Dating sucks when you're in a poor love situation

9. PEOPLE SKILLS   103
   Dating rocks when you get along well with others

10. SMALL TALK   115
    Dating rocks when men tune in to hear you speak

11. THE GOOD AUDIENCE   127
    Dating rocks when you're an outstanding listener

12. MEETING MEN   137
    Dating rocks when you attract lots of love prospects

CONTENTS

13. COMPETITION   147
Dating sucks when you battle too hard for attention

14. EARLY STAGES   157
Dating rocks when you control the pace and direction

15. LOVE CONNECTIONS   169
Dating sucks when you misjudge how well you click

16. PART-TIME BOYFRIENDS   179
Dating sucks when you limit your partner's interest

17. RELATIONSHIP CHALLENGES   189
Dating rocks when you handle problems effectively

18. ANGER MANAGEMENT   199
Dating sucks when you can't control your upsets

19. THE CERTAINTY PRINCIPLE   209
Dating rocks when you create convictions of the heart

20. AUTOMATIC EXCELLENCE   221
Love rocks when you maintain an attitude of gratitude

21. LOVING IS LIVING   231
Life rocks when you give with all of your heart

* ABOUT THE AUTHOR   238

* TODAY'S LOVE CHALLENGE   239

* BONUS SPECIAL REPORT   240

Introduction

"Mr. Nakamoto, you're going to be on in five minutes."

Those were the words of the assistant producer of the hit daytime television talk show *The Other Half* starring Danny Bonaduce, Dick Clark, Mario Lopez, and Dorian Gregory. It was a Tuesday afternoon in the summer of 2003, and I was standing backstage at NBC Studios in Burbank, California.

I had been invited there to talk to a national audience about my relationship book, *Men Are Like Fish: What Every Woman Needs to Know about Catching a Man*. At the time, *Men Are Like Fish* was the #1 best-selling dating-relationship book on Amazon.com, and the producers of *The Other Half* were looking for a fresh angle on the age-old topic of male/female romantic relationships.

But as the time for me to go on camera was ticking down, I had a sudden panic attack and ran off to the restroom to freshen up and compose myself. This was to be my first appearance on television before a live audience. I had been in a studio once to do a taping of a local cable show and had appeared on over 200 radio talk-shows. But being on a nationally televised talk-show in front of a live studio audience was a big first for me.

After a quick flash of time, I was positioned on stage behind a curtain. Soon the announcer introduced me by saying, "Have you been fishing for the perfect man only to find out that all the good ones have already been caught? Our next guest says that finding love starts with using the right bait. Ladies and gentlemen, please welcome Steve Nakamoto, the author of *Men Are Like Fish: What Every Woman Needs to Know about Catching a Man.*"

As I walked on stage, I waved to the audience of some 200. I then took a seat right next to Danny Bonaduce, who starred in *The Partridge Family* television series back in the early 1970s. Time is precious on television, so almost immediately Danny asked me, "So tell us Steve, how are men like fish?"

Even though I had been asked that same question hundreds of times, I drew an immediate blank. I was a little blown away by the bright lights and the three cameras that were focused on me as I tried to speak. However, somehow I managed to get started and went on to respond with my fully rehearsed answers to the 10 prearranged questions. Meanwhile, the hosts kept this challenging by repeatedly interrupting my flow of thought with their own little stories about dating and relationships. I began thinking, "Hey, this is my airtime that you guys are cutting into!"

The interview was moving along quickly, and I was in the middle of one of my little anecdotes when Danny interrupted me saying, "I'm sure that was a story for the ages. Thank you so much for being with us. Ladies and gentlemen, how about a hand for Steve Nakamoto."

A short time later, I drove home from the studio exhilarated because I got to fulfill one of my biggest dreams — performing on national television and overcoming my lifelong debilitating fear of public speaking.

BECOMING THE NEW "MR. ANSWER MAN"

Despite being seen on television by millions of viewers on *The Other Half*, I didn't sell many books in the days that immediately followed the appearance. I continued my promotion campaign by doing radio interviews on morning drive-time shows and sending my book to magazine writers who were in search of new quotable dating material. The book remained popular and sold at a steady rate.

Luckily for me, a magazine writer sent my book to the relationship department of iVillage.com, the world's largest online women's community. I quickly got an email and a phone call from the head of the editorial department, Francesca. She asked me if I would be interested in being the new host of the "Ask Mr. Answer Man" message board.

In September 2003, I accepted my role as the new "Mr. Answer Man." At first, there were about 20 questions a week. Initially, I wrote a full-page answer to each of these posted questions. But as the sheer number of questions increased, I had to develop some short cuts to writing my responses.

Around Valentine's Day, I logged on to find that I had 75 messages from posters on the "Ask Mr. Answer Man" message board. It took me about five days to respond to them all. At that point, I was starting to see that the same dating situations were coming up over and over again.

After six months of responding to hundreds of postings, I knew that I was hitting upon some rather obvious trends. As my approach became more refined and reflective of these trends, my advice to posters was consistently resulting in lots of positive feedback from the women who followed my suggestions. I could see that there are clear signposts in a relationship to which women could respond with the right move or the wrong move. If a woman responded with the wrong move, she would likely experience all of the pain, disappointment, and misery associated with failed love romances. But if she responded with the right move, this would lead her in the direction of successful relationships.

DATING ROCKS VS. DATING SUCKS

With time, I decided I wanted to share my new exciting discoveries about dating, romance, and love with more women through a new book. *Dating Rocks!* is my answer to the question "What has to happen in order to make love work?" I chose this focus because when love isn't working, dating can really suck! But when love does work, dating truly rocks!

"Sucks: Inadequate, displeasing, or poor quality."
The Online Slang Dictionary (1998)

Our culture is already filled with plenty of stories about how dating sucks. It's easy to identify with the struggles of frustrated, disappointed, and angry women. But for most women, the dream of true love still exists. And the best way to fulfill that dream is to build an empowering plan to achieve it rather than passively complaining about what's not right or fair.

Dating Rocks! is a book about ideas and inspiration. It is designed for the sensitive gal who wants to see beyond the limited and often damaging vision of love that more jaded women have. It's for the woman who wants to gain a productive view on how to make love work in her own life.

This is not a book for those unenlightened women who want to blame others for their dating failures. Nor is it for the damsels who simply choose to wait around for their Prince Charming to arrive in shining armor.

> "Rocks: To be very good, excellent, cool."
> *The College Slang Research Project* (1999)

As you read this book, I will constantly remind you that while dating sucks when your actions are misguided, short-sighted, and ultimately wasted, dating rocks when you finally discover the smart moves that make love work.

KEEP YOUR MIND READY FOR A LIFE-CHANGING IDEA

There's an old story about a visitor who walked into a temple and started asking questions of the resident Zen Master. Before the Zen Master could answer him, the man began spouting off his opinions about Enlightenment. As the visitor spoke, the Zen Master sat quietly and listened while pouring him a cup of hot tea.

To the visitor's amazement, the Zen Master continued pouring as the cup overflowed. The tea spilled all over the table and onto the floor.

The startled visitor asked the Zen Master, "Why are you continuing to fill up my cup after it is already full of tea?"

The Zen Master replied, "I am trying to show you that you are like this cup of tea. You are so full of your own preconceived notions that nothing else can go in. I cannot teach you about Enlightenment until you have first emptied out your cup."

As human beings sharing the amazingly complex journey of life, we each need to be reminded to put away our personal biases in order to glean the wisdom from a new source of information. Otherwise, we will only reinforce what we already know or believe to be true and reject anything that might be both fresh and useful.

THE MASTER STRATEGY: MAKE ONLY SMART MOVES

So the first key to dating enlightenment that I want to "pour into your cup" is this incredibly simple, and yet powerful philosophy:

Commit to making only smart moves.

I fully realize that there will invariably be some smart moves in your love life that won't give you the immediate results you want. I also suspect that an occasional dumb move may luck out for you or someone else that you know. But the important point that I want to make is that your consistent smart moves will lead you in the right direction toward succeeding at dating and relationships while a steady assortment of dumb moves simply won't.

We live in a period when advice on dating is given frequently and without restraint. I feel that what is most valuable about this book is not the information or principles of successful dating themselves. You can certainly find lots of great ideas from many other authors. But what I do believe is most important for you is to know clearly what is significant and what is trivial. With my help, you can stay focused on the majors issues in your love life, and let the minor things take care of themselves.

APPRECIATE THE VALUE OF A MALE PERSPECTIVE

Most women get their ideas about dating and love exclusively from the opinions of other women. However, a smart woman also realizes the difference between talking about love for entertainment only and discussing relationships with the purpose of gathering reliable information. Since men make up the other half of the love equation, a woman would be wise to also seek out the most accurate male perspectives on her important relationship challenges. That's where I come in.

My hope is that this book will help you make the smartest choices in your love life based on the best I have to offer. I'm sure there will be times when you'll be tempted to react in disgust by saying, "Isn't that spoken like a man!" But in the context of accurate feedback, an honest male perspective is an essential part of what you really do need.

By appreciating the value of a male viewpoint and consistently making only smart moves in your love life, you will be able to avoid the common pitfalls that most people encounter. Ultimately, this will help you towards the love relationship you truly desire.

Just remember to keep your unwavering faith during this entire process. Stay secure in the knowing that the universe mysteriously rewards those who show they are deserving through outstanding, purposeful action — not those who simply wish and hope.

Good luck on your personal journey to love, and may your new dating life truly rock!

"Crabs, sharks, octopi, jellyfish, shrimp... Reminds me of some of my dates."

Dating Rocks!

One

Dead-End Romances

DATING SUCKS WHEN IT GOES NOWHERE

"There are many ways of breaking
a heart. Stories were full of hearts being
broken by love, but what really broke
a heart was taking away its dream —
whatever the dream might be."

Pearl S. Buck
Author of *The Good Earth* (1931)

dead-end ro•mance: 1. a love relationship that never gets off the ground or one that goes nowhere and eventually dies out. 2. a frustrating, disappointing, and emotionally painful affair for both the man and the woman involved. 3. what smart women want to recognize and avoid in their love lives.

An honest male perspective: Clarity is powerful! You can't rely on solving your inevitable love challenges with luck or your good looks alone. You must acquire a solid knowledge base and interpersonal skill set in order to get from where you are presently to where you want to be in the future.

Did you ever see the light-hearted romantic comedy *What Women Want* starring Mel Gibson and Helen Hunt? It's a movie about a man who gets jolted by electricity and develops the unique ability to read women's minds. What I liked most about this movie was that it revealed a lot of interesting things about male and female behavior. The observations of screenwriters Josh Goldsmith and Cathy Yuspa are both amusing and truthful about our common search for love.

The basic premise of the movie is that men don't listen very well and therefore don't know what women want. This goes against a popular notion amongst men today that what the majority of women desire is obvious to us. Isn't it our masculine attributes and material riches first and foremost? Actually the truth is that a sensitive woman will value a man she relates to well and can trust over a man who is better looking or has more to offer financially.

THE "CHICKS DIG IT" MENTALITY

In the 1990s, I got this crazy idea that "chicks dig guys with power" — probably the result of getting caught up in the trendy and popular Tony Robbins "Fear into Power: The Firewalk Experience" seminars.

So I bought a used Porsche, a thousand-dollar suit with the corresponding red power tie, and proceeded to frequent all the upscale singles hotspots in Newport Beach, California.

Although the power theme seemed to work well in that phony environment, I eventually realized that it didn't take much to impress gullible women. Meanwhile, the more discriminating ones could see quite easily through my not-so-clever disguises and overly inflated ego. By using deceptive dating tactics, I was encouraging the kind of dead-end relationship that both the women and I wanted to avoid.

This was a positive realization on an even more practical level. Playing the power theme to attract women was just too expensive for my limited Average Joe budget.

WHAT DO WOMEN REALLY WANT?

One day in an effort to stimulate participation on iVillage.com's "Ask Mr. Answer Man" message board, I decided to post a discussion question which read: WHAT DO MOST WOMEN REALLY WANT IN THEIR LOVE LIFE?

Over the next week, I received 57 responses to my question from women all over the world. Their replies ranged from light ("I want a man who can vacuum.") to more serious ("I want a life partner I can trust.") and from cynical ("Is there a man out there who doesn't go to strip clubs?") to

What Women Say They Want

Here is a partial list of the type of things that women wrote when I asked the following question on iVillage.com's "Ask Mr. Answer Man" discussion board: "What do most women really want in their love life?"

* Someone who really wants to be the man in my life
* A man who listens carefully to what I say without judgment or advice
* A man who cheers me up when I am feeling down
* Someone who makes me feel very important to him
* A man who loves and respects me despite my personal flaws
* A man who will defend my honor when others try to put me down
* A man who is comfortable with who he is and is down-to-earth
* Someone who is honest and I can trust with all of my heart
* A sensitive man who is not afraid to say "I love you"
* A guy who doesn't try any cheesy pick-up lines on me
* A man with lots of money who isn't afraid to spend it on me
* A guy with good personal hygiene who takes care of himself
* A man who understands that women enjoy lots of romance
* A man who will show his emotions and even cry if appropriate
* Someone who is sensitive and observant to my changing moods
* A man who is mature, responsible, and dependable in tough times
* Someone who makes me laugh with his great sense of humor
* A man who actively helps me out without being reminded or nagged
* A man who is a challenge to me and not a pushover
* A guy who gives his full attention to me when I'm with him
* A man who makes me feel attractive and desirable with compliments
* A man who can carry on an interesting and intelligent conversation
* A man who is genuinely kind-hearted toward myself and others
* A man with good common sense and a thirst for knowledge
* A man who can spend lots of time with me without becoming antsy
* A man who is sexy, masculine, fun, playful, and a great lover
* A man with good manners and a refined sense of class and style
* A guy who respects my privacy and doesn't try to control me
* A man who is open and direct and willing to compromise if necessary
* A man who will love me, stay loyal, and not cheat

more enlightened ("It's not enough to be with someone who wants to be with me, that person has to be right for me as well.").

> **"Success and failure are both greatly overrated but failure gives you a whole more to talk about."**
> Hildegard Knef
> Author of *The Gift Horse* (1970)

Through my research, I've discovered that many women have lots of ideas about what they do and do not want in their love lives. However, women can have trouble recognizing whether a particular man and situation are right or wrong for them. It is my goal in this chapter to offer some insights that will help you steer yourself toward the right choices in the future.

THE PLEASURE-PAIN PRINCIPLE

During my years as a personal development trainer, I was taught that human behavior is controlled by two emotional forces that we commonly refer to as pleasure and pain.

Simply put, human behavior is based on people either seeking to gain pleasure or to avoid pain in their lives. Whatever a person chooses to do, consciously or unconsciously, he or she is controlled by either or both of these emotional driving forces. In regards to romantic relationships, men and women both have to be aware that they need to seek more pleasure and less pain in their lives. Importantly, and in addition, they also want to experience this emotional blend consistently over a long period of time.

While we may desire the pleasures of passion and romance

21

in the moment, more enlightened men and women are also hoping to experience sustainable, everyday love and, in most cases, a joyous and fulfilling marriage that lasts.

What Women Don't Want: Dead-End Romances

I love how one woman responded to my discussion question regarding what most women really want in their love life. This gal laid it on the line so clearly when she wrote the following about men she chooses not to date:

> "I hate to be negative about men, but here goes:
> How about no more staples through the nose,
> tongue, cheek, eyebrow, or whatever. And
> absolutely no more dirty ponytails that look like
> they haven't been washed in a year. While I'm at
> it, how about no more earrings of any kind. I also
> don't want a guy who calls everybody 'duuuude.'
> I'm also sick of guys who can't carry on a normal
> conversation without dropping a four-letter cuss
> word in every other sentence. But maybe it's just
> me who is the picky one because I see other
> women with these freaking jerks all of the time!"

Other women said that they didn't want to be in a relationship with someone who lies, cheats, or can't commit. They also don't want a situation in which there are major hassles with jealous ex-wives and previous girlfriends, or complicated family problems with children from a previous relationship. But most of all, like the above description implies, women don't want to be in a relationship that turns into a dead-end romance that leads nowhere.

Therefore, what every smart woman wants to avoid in her love life is a relationship with a man that has a lot of pain and very little pleasure. In order to achieve this objective, a woman has to be alert to the early dating signals that point in the direction of failure. And when these signals occur, she needs to make a clear-cut decision to pursue love in a different direction with a more suitable man and a better relationship situation.

What Women And Men Need: A Love That Works!

One of the roles that I've enjoyed over the years is being a professional tour director. Through the tours, I've taken people on first-class vacations all over the world! The majority of my tour clients are senior citizens who have the time, money, and desire to go on expensive sightseeing trips.

My unique position as a tour director has allowed me to observe how my clients interact with each other while on vacation. I remember one elderly couple in particular because they were laughing, having a great time, and being playful on our bus even though we were driving through a heavy rainstorm in the Canadian Rockies. These two were recently married after both of them had been widowed for many years. Because of delightful people like these two, I now appreciate how important companionship, communication, and caring are to love relationships, especially as the years pass by.

I'll also never forget one gentleman on a recent tour to Branson, Missouri. This fellow confided with me on a man-to-man basis by saying, "Steve, as a man's testosterone level declines, he begins to see his love life in a completely different way. In my early days, love was all about sex. As I've gotten older, love is more about sharing your life with someone you like and who understands you. Don't get me wrong, Steve. I still think sex is great. It's just not as important to me as it used to be."

In general terms, young men dream more about sex while young women dream more about romance. And it's important for a man or woman of any age to have dreams for their love life that motivates them. But as many wise men and women will attest, being willing to trade in your lustful adolescent dreams for a more joyful, everyday love relationship is something that make more sense as time goes by.

> "Nobody dies from lack of sex.
> It's lack of love we die from."
>
> Margaret Atwood
> Author of *The Handmaid's Tale* (1985)

What really rocks for many sensible women today is a romantic relationship that consistently works well and produces peace of mind and trust for both parties. The big thrill that doesn't last long is something that more women these days are finding less desirable.

SMART MOVE #1: KNOW WHAT IT TAKES TO SUCCEED

In order to experience a joyful love that works consistently and lasts, there needs to be *a blend of four critical ingredients.* Major problems start to crop up when one or more of these key relationship ingredients are missing. So for long-term success, be sure to combine all four in your relationships:

⑨ **The Right Woman.** Strengthen your relationship assets by becoming as attractive as you possibly can in the eyes of a man. Maximize your physical beauty, appeal to all of the senses, develop a more interesting personality, be able to stir him emotionally, become a more skilled conversationalist, and demonstrate the strength of character and the pureness of heart that earns you the respect, admiration, affection, and trust of men.

❧ **The Right Man.** This is a potential love partner with many attractive individual qualities and very few, if any, that are not appealing. In addition, be sure that you share mutually high levels of chemistry, common human values, compatible lifestyle habits, harmonious personalities, matching relationship goals, and the unique ability to bring out the best in each other. Remember, that the choosing of a mate will determine about 90% of your life's happiness or misery!

❧ **The Right Situation.** This occurs when both parties are free and clear of relationship obstacles such as lingering emotional attachments, unfriendly competition, and family problems. Avoid relationships that involve severe geographic challenges, divisive cultural perspectives, large age differences, vast class distinctions, and conflicting time schedules, to name a few.

❧ **The Right Tools.** Some ways to increase your personal assets in a love relationship include the following: make smarter decisions, design a more balanced lifestyle, stay physically fit and attractive, master your people skills, handle adversity more calmly, become a better talker and listener, manage your upsets, grow in emotional maturity, learn to be more fun-loving and cheerful, and stay true to your own interests without hurting others.

I've observed that both men and women dream of acquiring a new love relationship that promises the pleasures of driving passion, beautiful romance, supportive friendship, intimate connection, outrageous fun, personal growth, mutual gratitude, enhanced self-esteem, and complete peace of mind. In order for this to happen, a smart woman must become an irresistible, well-balanced love partner who attracts into her life the right man and the right situation. By doing this, she can take a promising dating situation and guide it naturally into the dream relationship that she's always wanted.

WHAT TO DO NOW

Take a moment now and think of a relationship in your past that eventually turned into a painful dead-end romance. Can you pinpoint whether the cause of failure in that relationship was primarily the man you chose, the situation you got involved in, or perhaps it was you and your personal makeup at the time?

Now do the same for other times in your romantic history. Can you find a pattern to your relationship failures? Do you tend to choose the wrong men or do you get yourself involved in too many low-percentage love situations? Or do your failures come in large part from being ill-equipped to handle adversity, adjust to change, or deal with uncertainty and instability in the relationship?

If your romantic failures were the result of a once-in-a-lifetime error, forgive yourself and move on to your next love opportunity. On the other hand, if you keep making the same types of mistakes in your love relationships, make sure that you pay special attention to your unwise tendencies. Then resolve to gain a deeper understanding of your particular challenges while you read through the following chapters. That way, you'll be preparing yourself to make the right choices, instead of the wrong ones, in your next romantic relationship.

> **"We fail to see that we can control our own destiny; make ourselves do whatever is possible; make ourselves become whatever we long to be."**
> Orison Swett Marden
> Author of *He Can Who Thinks He Can* (1908)

Getting clear on what it takes to succeed — and equally as important, what it takes to fail — are smart moves any woman can make. These insights will allow you to start to move towards the dream and achievement of love and happiness.

Like most things of lasting value in life, love is something that you deserve and earn by making the right choices. Indeed, enduring love is the result of following through with outstanding, consistent actions. It's not just a gift that life simply hands you.

THE BOTTOM LINE

Dating sucks when the abundance of pain or the lack of pleasure causes a relationship to go nowhere. But dating rocks when you begin combining the right man, the right woman, the right situation, and the right relationship tools together. This winning combination is necessary to create a love future that is filled with massive pleasure and little pain.

Two

Love Decisions

DATING ROCKS WHEN YOU
TAKE CHARGE OF YOUR LOVE LIFE

"Sow an act and you reap a habit;
sow a habit and you reap a character;
sow a character and you reap a destiny."

Frances E. Willard
American social reformer (1839-1898)

de•ci•sions: 1. reaching conclusions or passing judgments. 2. conscious and unconscious evaluations of things you think are significant, what they mean to you, and what actions to take. 3. in the context of romantic relationships, the series of moves that collectively result in shaping your love destiny.

An honest male perspective: Your decisions will either guide you towards or away from love! Make sure that you develop a reliable system for processing information and handling your emotions so that you stay on the right path towards the love you want.

"I'm going to crush my competition and I'm going to enjoy doing it," said Omarosa Manigault-Stallworth, a participant in NBC's hit reality show, *The Apprentice.* During its first season, *The Apprentice,* starring billionaire real estate mogul Donald Trump, became the network's #1 series of the season, with over 40 million viewers tuning in to the show's dramatic finale that year.

Omarosa became, perhaps, the most memorable of the show's participants who were competing at the time to win a dream job with The Trump Organization, and a hefty six-figure annual salary. Love her or hate her, one thing was for certain — Omarosa always created a big stir, regardless of the situation.

But during one of the final weeks of the competition, Omarosa became the target of Mr. Trump's famous line "You're fired!" and she was eliminated from the contest. Evidently, Trump grew tired of Omarosa's long line of excuses for her poor performances. Being a man of high achievement, Mr. Trump clearly does not tolerate making excuses for failure.

Likewise, as a smart woman looking to improve her love life, you should realize that making lame excuses for failure is a loser's strategy. However, taking full responsibility for your love life is one of the first key steps to moving rapidly towards a winning future.

YOU ARE PART OF THE LOVE EQUATION

This week, I received a private message from a discouraged woman who described her love life in the following way:

> "This past year, I've been really unlucky with my love life. First, I dated a drug addict who cheated on me behind my back. Next, I dated a man who would disappear on me and then come back out of the blue and expect to start where he left off. Another loser was an alcoholic who would pick fights and get violent with me. Then I fell for a guy who was crazy about me. But after the initial attraction, he became too needy and creepy-clingy. Can you please help me figure out my dating mess? I'm so tired of being this unlucky with men!"

In my reply, the point I tried to make was that she must realize her part in the equation. It isn't her luck that is making her date these men. After all, this woman is responsible for choosing to get involved with them in the first place. Perhaps she'd been going to undesirable meeting places and was associating with the wrong crowd, therefore she attracted these kinds of questionable characters. But mostly, it's important for her to know that the decisions she makes will ultimately determine the quality of her love relationships. Fortunately, she had the good sense to stop seeing these shaky suitors. As long as she can learn from her mistakes, this woman will be actively contributing to her likelihood of finding real love at last.

MEN BLAME IT ON BAD LUCK, TOO!

My friend Larry and I used to go to an upscale nightclub in Orange County, California called *The View*, where we always seemed to run into an overabundance of local "gold-diggers." He and I both had good success meeting women at this place — we'd get into great conversations, exchange phone numbers with potential dates, and maybe even sneak in a decent good-bye kiss. However, getting past a second date rarely happened with these women.

At first we blamed it on our bad luck of meeting "gold-diggers." But then another one of our friends summed up these experiences more bluntly. He said, "The problem isn't that these women are gold-diggers. It's just that you guys unfortunately can't afford them."

So rather than blaming our lack of success at finding love on gold-digging women, Larry and I proceeded to avoid high-profile meeting places like *The View*. Instead, we started doing other activities which didn't center around us trying to impress women in material ways.

Whether you're a man or a woman, it's always easier to blame others for your failures. But to take the enlightened path is to take full responsibility for your decisions, and consequentially accept the pain that goes along with taking necessary risks in your love life. These risks include trying new approaches to meeting someone. As you change, take heart in the common wisdom that suggests that the bigger the risk, the bigger the reward.

PLANT THE SEEDS OF FUTURE LOVE

What most people don't realize is that what happens in their lives is largely determined by the principle of cause and effect. But we usually only recognize the effects, which would include such things as a happy marriage, a nasty divorce, or not having any relationship at all. Rarely do people examine the causes which are the collective decisions we make in the relationship process.

It's true that luck can enter into the picture at any time during your pursuit of love. However, you are wise to acknowledge its periodic appearances, but foolish if you depend on luck entirely for your success. Most likely, the decisions you make will have the greatest influence on what kind of relationship you end up with — not luck.

A good way to illustrate the principle of cause and effect is through the analogy of planting seeds and reaping a harvest. For example, the actions we take create future results, just like seeds that eventually sprout into plants. If a person plants the seeds abundantly, and on good soil, that person can reasonably expect to reap an eventual harvest. But if a person doesn't plant the seeds abundantly, or chooses poor soil, they cannot expect to reap much of a crop.

In the case of love relationships, planting the seeds of love is usually a risky business with no guarantees of success. In pursuing relationships, you might plant the seeds of your good intentions (sincere appreciation, generosity, affection, patience, caring, and understanding) and still end up with instant rejection or eventual failure. But at the same time, you have to realize that if you don't risk planting any seeds, you will have absolutely no chance of reaping a harvest of love in the future.

The good news is that skillful planting can produce abundance! And, in the case of love, this is a bumper crop of good social opportunities, worthwhile connections, and excellent candidates for a fulfilling romantic relationship.

SMART MOVE #2: BECOME A GREAT DECISION-MAKER

To help you plant the seeds of better decisions, here are some keys points to remember for reaping a better harvest in your love life:

☙ **Develop more strength in your decision-making muscle.** Practice making decisions when the stakes are small. That way, you'll be ready to act when more significant decisions inevitably come your way. The quality of being a more decisive person develops naturally from repetition, and motivation will come from the goal of improving your love life. You'll become a great decision-maker through practice and a sense of a greater purpose.

☙ **Understand the proper role of luck.** A lasting love relationship is achieved by design — not by accident. That is not to say that luck isn't a factor, because it certainly can be — such as when it comes to meeting the right guy at the right time. But the foolish strategy is to rely solely on luck, instead of on skillful decision-making, which is the more dominant factor in achieving successful long-term results in love. A smart decision-maker allows for luck, but is never fooled by it.

❦ **Gain the value of insightful new perspectives.** With our human vision, having two eyes enables us to see with more depth. Likewise, when it comes to your love life, two perspectives will be better than one — and more can be even better! The mistake that most people make is to base their decisions exclusively on one point of view, which is usually their own or that of like-minded friends. Rarely do people consciously seek out opposing points of view about their love lives. I suggest that you consider the opinions of experts in the field, and perhaps the viewpoint of a well-informed and trusted member of the opposite sex. A wise decision-maker views an important issue at hand from at least three different sides.

❦ **Seek honest and accurate feedback.** In the area of dating, people can be especially sensitive about hearing honest feedback about themselves. Your close friends are not necessarily the best source of feedback about what you need to change in your actions and appearance. Often they will be afraid of hurting your feelings and damaging your friendship. But it is important to seek out honest feedback, so you can address the problem and not continue in the wrong direction.

❦ **Always stay flexible in your approach.** One of the hardest things for many of us to do is adjust to changing conditions. In other words, there comes a time when forcing things to happen is counterproductive, and learning to go with the flow will serve us better. Therefore, it is important to change our approach when things in our love lives aren't working, and realize that constantly repeating a bad strategy will continue to result in failure. A smart woman's approach is to take action, get feedback, and refine her dating strategies at various stages until she gets it right.

☺ **Don't make any significant decisions when you're upset.** Poor decisions about one's love life are often the result of making them while you're in an unresourceful, emotionally unstable state of mind. The plain truth is that we make gross errors in judgment, and make rash decisions when we're upset. The smart thing to do is to postpone a significant decision until you are in a more balanced frame-of-mind. An outstanding decision-maker knows that quality choices can best be made when a person's mind, body, and spirit are in perfect balance.

☺ **Remember to always do the right thing.** Some decisions are difficult to make and involve major consequences in our lives. The lazy habit that many people have is to choose what is the quickest, easiest, or least painful. But this decision-making process only creates a short-term quick fix. In order to make wise decisions over the long-term, you should carefully factor in these four important questions: (1) What is best for you? (2) What is best for the other person? (3) What serves the greater good? and (4) What is the most morally sound choice? When you have a balanced mental evaluation system like this, you will be guided towards doing the right thing.

Smart women don't leave their love lives entirely to chance. Instead, they shape their destiny by making wise decisions that serve their best interests. You can do the same by taking charge of your own love life and making the kinds of quality choices that naturally lead you away from relationship failure and frustration, and towards the high-quality love relationships that you truly desire and deserve.

What To Do Now

Take a moment and think of a time when you made a significant error in judgment. Based on the previous discussion, can you pinpoint the factors that contributed to the poor evaluation or decision you made at the time?

Realize that excellent decision-making requires you to study the consequences of your past actions and then to practice making decisions in better ways. Learn from your mistakes and accept full responsibility for your actions. Take charge of your love life by becoming a decisive person who knows that success in life comes naturally from our cumulative choices.

Women who do well in relationships are those who make their choices with their own best interests at heart. As a result, they can accept the results that come, and they don't have to explain away their failures with an endless chorus of weak excuses.

The Bottom Line

Dating sucks when you feel like you don't have any control over the quality of your love life and it seems like things just happen to you. But dating rocks when you make a conscious decision to take charge of your destiny. You can take charge *now* by learning how to make intelligent choices that will lead you towards true lasting love.

Three

The Power Source

DATING ROCKS WHEN YOU LOVE YOURSELF FIRST

"I have an everyday religion that
works for me. Love yourself first
and everything else falls into line.
You really have to love yourself
to get anything done in this world."

Lucille Ball
American actress-comedian (1911-1989)

self-es•teem: 1. how highly you regard or value yourself. 2. the opinions or judgments that you hold for yourself. 3. in the context of love relationships, the source of power that starts inside of an individual and radiates out to others.

An honest male perspective: Love always begins with you! You must love yourself first in order to love others. Love is a two-way street of giving and receiving. You can't give away the gift of love unless you possess it within yourself in the first place. And you can't receive and accept love if you don't feel deep inside that you deserve it.

Haven't we all seen the television commercials that feature the pink bunny who wears cool shades, plays a drum, and keeps on "going and going and going"?

Of course, I'm referring to the famous Energizer Bunny®. Ever since 1989, he has been capturing people's attention around the world as the advertising icon of long-lasting Eveready Energizer® batteries.

For women looking to persist in their quest for true love, they also need to find an unstoppable, ever-present emotional power source that keeps them "going and going and going" through the inevitable challenges and setbacks in romantic relationships.

LOW SELF-ESTEEM DESTROYS LOVE

A guy wrote the following to me about how his girlfriend's low self-esteem was dragging their relationship down:

"My girlfriend constantly needs reassurances of
how I feel about her. She seems to believe that I
will leave her for someone better and has actually
voiced those exact concerns to me. Because of this, I
have to make a conscious effort to be more affection-
ate towards her, but it really doesn't seem to help
any. Don't get me wrong. I truly adore my girlfriend. After all, she's my first love and, as a person,
she has a lot of wonderful qualities. But I am reaching that critical point where I just can't take it anymore. What constructive advice can you give me
about helping my girlfriend boost her self-esteem so
our relationship can be fun again for both of us!

The case above illustrates how having low self-esteem can
have multiple negative effects. First, it is unattractive to
potential love partners because it brings them down emotionally. Second, having low self-esteem prevents a woman
from performing at her best. And finally, when someone has
a low opinion of themselves, they send an unconscious message out to others that there must be something wrong with
them. In all of these instances, low self-esteem brings love to
a halt while high self-esteem would have allowed love the
chance to keep on going.

BE A SELF-ESTEEM BUILDER, NOT A WRECKER

Back in high school, I used to pick on an egotistical surfer
kid named Charles Krieger. I even went so far as to write a
sarcastic poem for my 10th grade English class about his fic-
titious demise. The title of the poem was "Charles Krieger's
Last Good-Bye," and it told the story of one foggy morning
when a group of us went surfing in dangerous ocean condi-

tions. For added humor, I sang the poem out loud to the tune of the theme song for the *Gilligan's Island* TV show.

The final verses of "Charles Krieger's Last Good-Bye" read as follows:

The sea started getting stormy
The smart guys paddled in to flee,
The only surfer out there
Charles Krieger named was he.

An ugly wave with snaring teeth
Eleven stories high,
"I'm the world's greatest surfer!"
Was Charles' last good-bye.

Back in those days, I mistook cockiness for confidence or high self-esteem. The honest truth is that I purposely tried to knock Charles Krieger down a few notches because he was more popular than me with the girls I liked.

My behavior in high-school towards kids like Charles Krieger indicated that I had more cockiness than actual self-confidence. While it may have looked the same from the outside, tearing down others wasn't a valid method of building my own sense of worthiness.

Whether you're a man or a woman, putting down others to make yourself feel more attractive is not a sustainable or desirable method for empowering your life. Choose a more enlightened approach to living life instead by building other people up and thereby raising your own self-esteem as a natural by-product. And further heighten your confidence and self-esteem by improving your personal foundation wherever it's weak.

YOUR LOVE POWER COMES FROM HIGH SELF-ESTEEM

Above all, a woman's true power source comes from loving herself. I'm sure that a lot of people will quickly say that they love themselves, while in reality they weaken their own power in unintentional and often overlooked ways like negative self-talk. Therefore, a more accurate gauge of a woman's true level of self-love is to add up all the good ways she treats herself and subtract away the things that she habitually does to diminish her own positive feelings of self-worth.

In order to attract love into your life, the first place to start is by improving the relationship you have with yourself. By doing this, you'll be sending out an unmistakable signal to the universe that you are a woman of incredible value, and any man would be crazy not to love and cherish you.

SMART MOVE #3: LOVE YOURSELF FIRST AND FOREMOST

Here are some ideas that will help boost your self-esteem and thereby strengthen your power source to give and receive love:

☞ **Rediscover your overlooked personal strengths**. There is a popular saying that goes, "It ain't bragging if it's true." In your private moments, be sure to take some time out to remember some of your often-overlooked positive qualities. Why wait around for someone else to give you an uplifting and empowering personal compliment, when nobody knows you better than you do? When your personal power starts to run low, be the first one to do a little bragging in the name of love.

"It seems apparent to me that your daughter is happy
as she is... and if you don't cut this out, Mother,
I'm going to start charging you for these visits!"

⊛ **Stop living to please others**. Most of us were raised to try to please other people, whether it was our parents, teachers, coaches, friends, or other family members. But as adults, there is a limit to how much energy we can spend on pleasing others before it is at the expense of our own desires. You can show how much you truly love yourself by choosing to prioritize your own needs over those of others. After an initial adjustment, this strategy will end up freeing up more positive energy in your life, which other people will find naturally attractive.

⊛ **Practice more compassion for others**. When we put ourselves in other people's shoes and feel empathy for their challenges, we are practicing compassion. This emotion helps us to open up our hearts and value other people. Even a small act, like looking people in the eye and saying "hello," sends a clear message to that other person that they matter. A simple, yet profound principle to remember is that you can't elevate another person's self-esteem without also elevating your own.

⊛ **Learn to laugh at yourself**. We would all agree that having a great sense of humor is attractive to others. And when we are able to direct this humor toward ourselves, it offers multiple benefits. First, it acts like a safety valve and takes off some of the pressure of everyday living. Secondly, it prevents us from taking ourselves too seriously. Also, it can prevent us from being too hard on ourselves when we don't measure up to our own high expectations. Lightening things up has the attractive side-benefit of putting others at ease, too! They don't have to worry that we'll be too hard on them also.

Positive Things You Can Say To Boost Your Self-Esteem

Here is a list of things that you can say to yourself in order to build your self-esteem. Your ability to rediscover and reaffirm your best human qualities will greatly affect how much you truly like and respect yourself. The more often you repeat this exercise with emotional intensity and congruent physiology, the more immune you will be to the negative comments of others. That way, you'll naturally become more attractive to everyone including the opposite sex.

* When you get right down to it, I really like myself.
* People like me because I put them at ease with my sense of humor.
* I respect myself because I am a person who keeps her word.
* People like me because of my natural enthusiasm.
* I like myself because I'm a hard, dedicated worker.
* People appreciate the fact that I am a really good listener.
* People trust me because I am honest and caring.
* I admire how well I can keep my own composure under pressure.
* I like my body and treat it well with exercise, rest, and a healthy diet.
* I love to help other people in any way that I can.
* Saying "no" to a request for my time gives that time back to me.
* I have a great smile that sends a good spirit out for others to enjoy.
* I'm really good around the house and especially in the kitchen.
* I've got good tastes when it comes to clothes and accessories.
* I may be stubborn, but on the other hand I'm persistent and thorough.
* When I take on calculated risk, I prove how much courage I have.
* I never lose as long as I learn something valuable from an experience.
* I gladly forgive others so I can release myself of all the negative energy.
* I appreciate and respect the uniqueness of other people.
* I'm forever young because I'm growing and searching for new ideas.
* I've done the best that I can with the resources that I've had at the time.
* No one can make me feel inferior unless I give them my permission.
* My will is bigger than anything that happens to me.
* There is always a way if I am courageous, persistent, and flexible.
* The more grateful I am, the more powerful I become.
* I'm such a unique person that I'm irreplaceable.

❧ **List your personal breakthroughs**. We all have proud moments when we were able to overcome a particular challenge successfully. Taking an inventory of these breakthrough moments and appreciating our progress can raise our self-esteem. For example, I experienced a personal breakthrough when I appeared on the NBC television talk-show *The Other Half* (mentioned previously in this book). For a guy whose biggest fear was public speaking, this was a feat that I'm still very proud of today. What accomplishments are you most proud of? Make sure that you create a list of your breakthroughs and put it somewhere where you can look at it regularly. Remind yourself of how wonderful and courageous you truly are.

❧ **Stop the critic inside you**. There is an internal voice within each of us that likes to remind us of our fears and limitations. When faced with a major challenge, this voice will often proclaim, "No you can't!" So it is our responsibility and duty to quiet that self-sabotaging voice. Listen instead to the powerful inspiration of your own inner and outer voice with repeated positive statements like "Yes, I can!" and "If it's to be, it's up to me." When possible, do this in front of a mirror. By reinforcing the message that you send yourself with strong tonality, sincere emotion, and congruent facial expressions, you'll be replacing your inner critic with a private cheerleader. This is a great way to raise and maintain a high self-esteem.

❧ **Get comfortable with your own body**. It's also important to accept and appreciate yourself on a physical level. While we can't all have "the perfect body," it's a good practice to remove any awkwardness or shyness that we may have with ourselves. A constructive thing to do is to stop thinking about how flawed your body looks and to start paying attention to how healthy your body is becoming. The healthiness of your body is something that you can have immediate control over through diet, discipline, exercise, and relaxation. And the bottom line is that a healthy body is a sexy body, which is all you really need to convey to men and, more importantly, to yourself.

☙ **Accept compliments graciously.** Many people have difficulty accepting compliments. They will often respond by lowering their heads or saying something to minimize the compliment. The internal effect is that you rob yourself of the self-esteem boost that you could be receiving from the other person. Instead of rejecting the next compliment, be ready to accept it graciously by holding your head high and saying, "Thank you." Do this and you will also allow the sender of the compliment to enjoy the gift of giving.

☙ **Treat yourself to well-deserved rewards.** It is a healthy practice to reward yourself periodically with special treats. That way, you'll be sending a clear message to yourself that you deserve to be treated well. If you don't feel worthy of accepting rewards in life, how can you expect another person to feel that you're worthy of their attention and love? Small indulgences like a trip to the spa for a facial and massage may do more than just make your body feel better. Such special treatment revitalizes the essential spirit of self-esteem, and it will power your love life.

By following these simple guidelines, a smart woman can create and maintain a healthy self-esteem and keep herself energized throughout her journey to love.

WHAT TO DO NOW

Take a moment now and think of one specific way in the past that you've unintentionally lowered your self-esteem. Maybe you've been far too critical of yourself or perhaps you've been someone who hasn't been able to accept compliments graciously. Can you see how that kind of habitual action would make you less attractive to prospective suitors? Now resolve to respond in only positive, empowering ways in the future.

When it comes to building and maintaining your self-esteem, why wait for tomorrow? What can you do right now in order to increase your love for yourself? Is there a well-deserved reward that you need to treat yourself to today? Is there a personal strength that you can write down this moment and savor for yourself?

> "Women who set low value on themselves
> make life hard for all women."
> Nellie L. McClung
> Author of *In Times Like These* (1915)

Looking out for "Number One" makes perfect sense, especially when it comes to increasing your value to others and putting yourself in the position to give and receive love.

THE BOTTOM LINE

Dating sucks when you're scaring men away inadvertently with your low self-esteem and self-destructive behavior. But dating rocks when you love yourself first and send out a clear signal to prospective men that you're a special woman who rightly deserves to be recognized, appreciated, and loved.

Four

Excess Baggage

DATING SUCKS WHEN THE PAST WEIGHS YOU DOWN

"She stayed bound to a gone moment,
like a stopped clock with hands silently
pointing to an hour it cannot be."

Elizabeth Bowen
Author of *The House in Paris* (1935)

bag•gage: 1. the suitcases, luggage, and parcels which one carries their belongings in while traveling. 2. the memories of the past that a person consciously or unconsciously carries around which still control their present emotions and actions. 3. the unnecessary weight of a woman's past that slows her down on the journey to love.

An honest male perspective: Emotional baggage is a HUGE turnoff to prospective love partners! A smart woman knows that she must do all she can to get rid of her emotional baggage. That way, she will possess the refreshing spirit that men universally find so attractive.

Today airlines are more likely to charge their customers an extra fee for baggage that exceeds a certain weight limit. Just before a recent flight, the suitcase that I brought along weighed in at 62 pounds. The airline representative at the check-in counter announced, "There will be an additional $25 service charge for going over the weight limit by twelve pounds." I realized too late that I would be penalized for carrying around excessive or heavy baggage.

In a similar way, a woman can be penalized in her love life for carting around too much emotional weight from her past. This happens when she uses past experiences in romantic relationships and elsewhere as the excuse for her present unhappiness and allows herself to remain stuck in a funk. A smart woman recognizes this danger and avoids it so that she can move around more freely in her future love relationships to the delight of prospective suitors.

WILL THE PAST ALWAYS REPEAT ITSELF?

One of the more common stories that I've read from women who post messages at iVillage.com is how a certain man in their past hurt them and now they can't trust new men. These women will say that all present and future love candidates will have to pay the price of doubt because of what another man did earlier.

For example, a woman wrote the following to me about her lack of trust for men:

> "I am at the point where I have absolutely no trust in men, their intentions, or their apparent interest in me anymore. I would like to know some key things I can look for that will give me a reason to believe a man isn't going to drop me and run like all the rest have. Recently, on two separate occa- sions, I met someone that I immediately clicked with. They both asked for my number, told me a time they'd call, and then I never heard from them again. They were both genuinely interested in me, from what I could tell, so I am at a loss as to when to believe someone when they say they'll call me. Because of these and other experiences, I just don't trust men. Can you offer me any advice?"

What I tell a woman with this kind of reasoning is that the past is only real because she chooses to continually refer to it. By habitually accessing a negative event from former times, the woman remains anchored to a set of circum- stances that doesn't necessarily apply to her present situa- tion. She is deciding by her way of thinking to carry the emo- tional weight of her past well into the future. In many cases, this kind of emotional baggage will scare away future dating prospects in the woman's life.

THERE'S DANGER IN GOOD MEMORIES, TOO!

Sometimes a good memory that is too well remembered becomes an obstacle to developing a new romance. The fondly held memories can limit appreciation for new experiences in the present.

There was a time when I had one of the most exciting and memorable romances aboard a cruise ship in the Caribbean. That shipboard fling transformed into a long-distance romance that lasted a few years before eventually dying out. But the good memories of that love affair lived on well past its appropriate and healthy expiration date.

Many years later, I was chatting with an old acquaintance of mine. Eventually he asked me, "What's your love life like these days, Steve?"

I remember that my reply included comments about the cruise-ship romance. My friend gave me a serious look and then responded, "Wasn't that like six or seven years ago? Are you still talking about that same cruise-ship fantasy of yours? Don't you think it's about time for you to get over it?"

I didn't particularly like my friend's remarks, but deep inside I knew he was right. I had been inadvertently holding on to a romantic dream with all of its hopes and impossible expectations. As a result, the reality was that I was stuck in the trap of the past. Those wonderful memories were making my present life look pale in comparison. For a long time, I hadn't been giving my real love-life a fair chance to succeed.

THE PAST IS *NOT* THE FUTURE UNLESS....

One useful realization is that the past will *not* be your future *unless* you choose to still live in it. If you quit using the past as an excuse for not giving your all, you can move forward freely in your life.

Every person can find a story to justify not being all they can be in their life today. But while some people use their stories to keep themselves stuck in an old mindset, others have found a way to let the past inspire them to new heights.

> "The past can seldom be recalled without sadness,
> for it was either better or worse than the present."
> Leonora Christina
> Danish princess and writer (1621-1698)

When you come to think about it, the past is nothing more than a memory that we decide to carry around with us. It is easily within our power to choose between carrying that memory around incessantly, lightening its emotional load or, if necessary, leaving it behind. We can do this by either changing our mental focus to the present or by changing the meaning and significance we attach to the past.

SMART MOVE #4: DON'T LET THE PAST ENSLAVE YOU

Experience can carry an emotional price and that price is often paid in full by the pain of regretfulness that we continue to suffer. But in order for us to stop punishing ourselves and move forward in our love lives, we must find an empowering value in our past so it can start serving us well in the future.

The following are strategies that are designed to help you lighten your emotional load or convert past experiences into more valuable assets for you to reinvest into your future:

🕮 **Convert your past pain into warnings**. If you can learn something from your past experiences, they have value

55

you can put to use today and in the future. When a decision results in negative consequences, then that experience becomes a warning not to choose that same course of action again. With this simple mindset adjustment, you can start to steer away from repeating your mistakes.

🌢 **Let your past pleasure inspire you to experience more.** When we recognize something good that happened in our past, it can serve to inspire us to experience that again. Instead of warnings, these pleasurable moments can be examples of how life rewards you when the right choices and circumstances come together. Remembering your successes can help restore your faith in love and your ability to attract it again into your life.

🌢 **Forgive yourself by adding the key missing resources.** Many of our past mistakes could have been avoided if we had the benefit of knowing the consequences in advance. The truth is that people do about the best they can with the mental, physical, and emotional resources that they have at any given time. By considering how a key present resource — like your current level of self-confidence — might have changed the outcome of a past experience, you can easily forgive yourself and let go of unnecessary and destructive emotional pain.

🌢 **Put a new empowering label on your old experience.** We have a tendency to describe a past event with an emotional label. For example, we will say something like "It was a humiliating experience." Now that may have been true when it happened, but for now you can constructively say that it was a "learning experience." That way, you can recall what you learned rather than how it felt to be humiliated. Another thing you can do is to describe this humiliating experience from the past as "a tad embarrassing" in retrospect. By describing your past with less emotionally charged words, you can access the event without bringing up the same intensity of pain.

☙ **Throw away all of the old anchors.** Sometimes it takes bold, radical moves to break the habit of hanging on to negative emotional feelings. In the case of forgetting painful relationships, it may be useful to toss out old photos, love letters, and romantic cards or gifts. It may also help to stop listening to songs of that time period which bring you back instantly to those lost moments. These reminders may be keeping you attached emotionally to unwanted and outdated times in your life and thus prevent you from appreciating what could be in your life today or in the future.

☙ **Get help if you need it.** If you need professional help to move forward, seek counsel from a goal-oriented therapist or life coach. Also, a weekly support group can help you realize that we all face challenges in our lives and let you see how others are handling theirs. In addition, techniques like breath work are useful for letting go of lingering difficult feelings. Lastly, remember that we all need to take a break from love at times after a relationship has been particularly painful. Perhaps this is a period when you can just date for fun, taking your time before getting too serious.

☙ **Don't look back, look forward instead.** Once you've been able to embrace the lessons of your past, control your focus by thinking, talking, and referring to things in your present. Think of the positive possibilities life could offer you today. Realize that when the mind doesn't have anything good to focus on in the present or for the future, it has a natural tendency to drift back to emotional events of the past. Also, if you fill your upcoming schedule with an assortment of worthwhile activities to experience, there won't be any time to obsess about the past.

🌷 **Give yourself a new adult identity.** How about becoming an "enlightened woman" now instead of continuing to be a "victim" of the past? All you have to do is willingly accept full responsibility for your love life, learn from every experience, and appreciate the healing process of becoming more compassionate toward yourself and others. By seeing yourself as living at a higher level, you can instantly lessen the pain of the past and make your general attitude more attractive to others.

🌷 **Remember to love yourself at all times.** Having high self-esteem is perhaps the greatest aid to repairing a hurtful past. The more you love and honor yourself, the more you'll be control of your own emotions. In addition, you'll feel less at the mercy of unpleasant circumstances — both in the past and present. The next time you come face-to-face with a hurtful reminder of your past, be sure to have incredible compassion for yourself. Also appreciate your newfound ability to handle challenges.

How you feel about your past will greatly affect your attitude towards your future love-life. As soon as you're ready, lighten up your emotional load so that you can be free to love again in the future. Don't penalize your love-life by hanging on to unnecessary and destructive memories from your past.

What To Do Now

Take an inventory of your past. What are the four or five most significant emotional events in your life? Perhaps your list includes the loss of a family member, an embarrassing incident that you experienced in school, a peak moment when you fell in love for the first time, or a difficult betrayal in a love relationship.

For each incident, find an empowering lesson. For example, I remember standing in front of a large crowd in junior high-school and forgetting the speech I was supposed to give. Looking back on that experience, I can now see how I was inspired to take public-speaking courses in order to avoid embarrassing myself in that way again.

So what are your stories and what could you gain from them? Be sure to do this for important incidents that are the source of unresolved issues in your life. Write down things in your past that you need to resolve and then deal with them head-on in the days ahead. Realize that it's not what happened to you that matters. It's what you do with the past that's important.

The Bottom Line

Dating sucks when your past weighs you down and makes your spirit less attractive to prospective men. But dating rocks when you discover how your past can help you grow into a human-being who has more love and compassion to give to the deserving men in your future.

LOW SELF ESTEEM
Bad Manners
Loquacity
EGO
CRITICAL
Jealousy
DISHONEST
LOUD
MOODY
Poor Hygiene
CONCEIT
Cynical
Vanity
GREED
xenophobic
STUBBORN

Five

Blind Spots

DATING SUCKS WHEN YOU DON'T KNOW YOUR WEAKNESSES

"Faults often talk louder than virtues."

Florence Crannell Means
Author of *A Candle in the Mist* (1931)

blind spot: 1. a part of an area that can't be clearly seen. 2. a subject about which a person is markedly ignorant, uninformed, prejudiced, or unaware. 3. in the context of this book, a woman's personal weakness that is apparent to everyone else except herself.

An honest male perspective: Your weaknesses can spook men away early and you will usually never know why they quit seeing you. That's why it is your responsibility to search hard and repair the things that make you less attractive to potential suitors.

When I think of women's blind spots, I can't help but recall an experience I personally had many years ago. As luck would have it, I met a beautiful woman at my gym. We both had taken the same aerobics class, and when I accidentally bumped her arm near the water fountain, she turned my way. During the workout, I had noticed that this woman was attractive, but now she was even more so. After all that exercise, her pretty face was naturally glowing with health and vitality. We got into a great conversation, and to my delight, she agreed to give me her phone number.

Boy, did this woman surprise me later that week, when I met her at a restaurant near the beach for a lunch date. She had packed on so much makeup that I couldn't decide whether she looked more like a clown or Tammy Faye Baker. Her heavy load of makeup was such a turnoff that I just politely got through the lunch, but never called her again. I couldn't help but wonder how she could ever believe that her makeup style was attractive. Instead, it was a blind spot for her — a factor that could turn men off, when she was obviously trying very hard to entice them.

Regardless of whatever blind spots you may have, it's important that you identify and take care of them so that the impressions you make on other people can be the most favorable. Remember, just one blind spot — like my date's heavy makeup — can cancel out several positive traits when it comes to the delicate art of dating.

Seek Out Accurate And Honest Feedback

When women continually suffer from failures in their love lives, they often start believing that there is something mysteriously wrong with them. More often than not, they are blind to their own characteristics that may be chasing men away.

I usually advise these women to seek honest feedback from a close and trusted friend. But this can be a worthless exercise if preserving the friendship overrules giving straight-forward and direct input. Because these issues are hard to discuss, it can end up being the man himself who reveals the woman's blind spot for her. Here's one woman's experience:

> "After our second date, Mike told me it really bothered him that my breath, clothes, and apartment smelled like cigarette smoke. Mike said that if he didn't like me so much, he would have just quit seeing me without saying anything about it. I was shocked because I'd already slept with him. Mike told me that if I saw the potential in our relationship that he recognized, I'd have to find a way to quit smoking. I had no idea that this was a

problem and I quickly went on nicotine patches so I could change all this. I'm really grateful that he told me because we've been together now for two years. Plus I've given up the nasty habit of smoking. I think a man needs to tell a woman this kind of personal stuff and know that we women don't get mad if it's done tactfully."

If you can't get honest accurate feedback from anyone, then I suggest that, much like a mechanic who inspects your car, you operate from a checklist. For example, a typical auto mechanic will check items like the engine oil, air filter, spark plugs, tire pressure, and brake fluid in a routine inspection. By going through his checklist of key items, a mechanic can make sure that nothing significant gets overlooked that can lead to costly negative consequences later on.

Similarly, a smart woman can create her own checklist of personal items (see The Blind Spots Checklist ahead on page 66 for ideas) to make sure that she doesn't overlook a glaring weakness that may be single-handedly destroying her immediate chances for love and romance.

Notice What Others Say About You

Another good way to locate a potential blind spot is to be acutely aware of what other people say about you in casual conversations.

I remember a time when a friend got frustrated with me and blurted out, "Steve, you're such a bleeping 'know-it-all.'" I had also heard a similar comment several years earlier, and upon hearing it again, realized that I could still come across that way to other people.

Armed with this renewed awareness, I toned down this unflattering aspect of my personality by admitting my ignorance from time to time on a few subjects openly. To prevent flare-ups of resentment, I also try to avoid bragging about my knowledge, speaking in a condescending tone, and annoying people with unwanted, unsolicited advice.

SMART MOVE #5: FIND AND FIX YOUR BLIND SPOTS

It's your strengths that cause men to be attracted to you and eventually fall in love. But it can be a grating weakness that will cause someone to limit their relationship with you or fall out of love. Make sure that you develop your personal gifts in order to attract people into your life. Just remember to be equally aware about taking care of your weaknesses so that the people you attract are willing to stay around.

To help you handle your major weaknesses, here are seven common blind spots that women need to be more aware of when it comes to creating dating success:

☺ **Share your smile openly.** A recent survey found that singles rate a person's smile and eyes as the most important features. So remember to share your smile frequently and freely with others. Also, be aware of providing good eye contact without overdoing it.

☺ **Get in great physical shape.** Exercise regularly by going to the gym, taking outdoor walks, or participating in your favorite sport. These kinds of physical activities have a positive impact on your mood as well as your form. Beyond improving your mood, the endorphins provided with exercise also help you have more energy to invest back into

The Blind Spots Checklist

FIND AND FIX ANY GLARING WEAKNESSES

• Beauty & Physique	Poor	Fair	Good
• Brains & Common Sense	Poor	Fair	Good
• Fitness & Vitality	Poor	Fair	Good
• Hair & Nails	Poor	Fair	Good
• Skin Quality	Poor	Fair	Good
• Body Posture	Poor	Fair	Good
• Breath Protection	Poor	Fair	Good
• Body Odor	Poor	Fair	Good
• Self-Confidence & Poise	Poor	Fair	Good
• Conversational Charm	Poor	Fair	Good
• Sense of Humor	Poor	Fair	Good
• Style & Dress	Poor	Fair	Good
• Sexiness & Femininity	Poor	Fair	Good
• Manners & Politeness	Poor	Fair	Good
• Ability to Laugh & Enjoy	Poor	Fair	Good
• Enthusiasm & Optimism	Poor	Fair	Good
• Spontaneity & Fun	Poor	Fair	Good
• Respect for Being on Time	Poor	Fair	Good
• Pleasant Voice Qualities	Poor	Fair	Good
• Warmth & Kindness	Poor	Fair	Good
• Ability to Listen & Learn	Poor	Fair	Good
• Easy to Please	Poor	Fair	Good
• Sense of Gratitude	Poor	Fair	Good
• Generosity	Poor	Fair	Good
• Ability to Manage Upsets	Poor	Fair	Good
• Responsibility & Maturity	Poor	Fair	Good
• Ability to Handle Stress	Poor	Fair	Good
• Honesty & Integrity	Poor	Fair	Good
• Basic Financial Stability	Poor	Fair	Good

THE BOTTOM LINE

What you don't know about yourself can hurt you in the dating marketplace. Do all you can to get the most honest and accurate feedback. Then make the necessary adjustments.

your social life. Getting in shape and being healthy are attractive qualities that send out a clear signal that you're taking care of yourself, and they provide a positive boost to your all-important self-esteem.

🕙 **Balance out your personality quirks.** Having an unflattering nickname may be a harmless thing among your inner circle of girlfriends, but it usually isn't an asset to have as your label in your love life. People often acquire nicknames because of radical imbalances in their personality or lifestyle. If you're being characterized in an unflattering way with nicknames like "Airhead," "Know-It-All," or "Blabbermouth," then it is best to neutralize this quickly. Start by mixing in some noticeable counter-balancing positive behavior and stick with it until you've outgrown the negative patterns as much as possible.

🕙 **Check your personal hygiene.** In grade school, kids make fun of people who have "B.O." (body odor). But as adults looking to make a great first impression, having body odor or bad breath is no laughing matter. Awareness and personal attention to your body are the first keys to handling these conditions. Don't wait for other people to be forced to tell you.

🕙 **Take care of your own basic needs.** Being desperate, a universal turnoff, is caused by having too many unfulfilled emotional needs. Love seems to work out best when the two parties involved come together as whole people looking to add to each other's lives. This is in contrast with being needy predators looking to latch on to someone. The best strategy for attracting and keeping love is to become emotionally balanced before entering into a new relationship. On the other hand, being an immediate emotional or financial drain on a new relationship partner can cause a quick, unannounced withdrawal.

☻ **Associate with the right crowd.** You are often judged by the company you keep. If you hang around a bunch of losers, then people will naturally assume that you're one also. I'm not saying that you can't benefit from having a wide variety of friends from different walks of life. What I am saying is that it makes more sense to limit your association with people who bring out the worst in you and expand your association with those who bring out the best. Don't make the common mistake of underestimating the power of influence and how your associations affect many aspects of your life.

☻ **Clean up your language.** Under stress, it is natural for people to be at their worst. We often express ourselves in this state with emotionally charged words and phrases. While it is sometimes more acceptable for men to utter ugly four-letter words or show public displays of anger, the double standards in our society can make it unforgivable for women who choose to do the same. The smart thing for women to do is make sure that they're discreet about their choice of words in public so that they don't lose unnecessary points for poor social manners.

By finding and fixing these common blind spots, you can avoid making costly first impression mistakes. Play it smart by making sure that your most visible personal features are not working against you so that the beauty of your true self has a fair chance to shine.

What To Do Now

Take a moment and go through the checklist of personal blind spots on page 66. Highlight the items that have the possibility of being somewhat true. Have a discussion with a friend about this checklist and see what they think about your items of concern. In a light-hearted way, sneak in a comment about how you're considering a few of these as possible problems and that you want their honest-to-God opinion. You can also pose this as a hypothetical question and ask, "If you were a guy, what would you think?" Brace yourself for their feedback, but realize that this is one of the least painful and most accurate ways of finding your blind spots.

Locating your blind spots can be the difficult part. Fixing them is often only a matter of raising your standards in that area, focusing on effective solutions, and following through with decisive action.

Remember that most people don't have to change a ton of things in order to get and keep the love they desire. More often than not, people need to make only one or two minor adjustments on the surface. In addition, there may be a couple trouble areas in your personal behavior that need some work. However, the effort will be well worth it when you make a connection that lasts.

The Bottom Line

Dating sucks when you have personal weaknesses that everyone recognizes except you. But dating rocks when you find and fix your weaknesses so that your strengths stand out more than anything to your love prospects.

Six

Irresistible Women

DATING ROCKS WHEN
MEN FIND YOU DESIRABLE

"A man falls in love through his eyes,
a woman through her imagination,
and then they both speak of it as
an affair of the heart."

Helen Rowland
Author of *A Guide to Men* (1922)

ir•re•sist•ible: 1. the inability to oppose, withstand, or keep from temptation. 2. having an overpowering appeal. 3. in the context of dating, a woman that every man desires to love.

An honest male perspective: Variety is the spice of love and life! The more ways you can be appealing to another person, the more interested they will be in you. When it comes to dating men, make sure that you show them many facets of your personality. That way, boredom doesn't become an important concern for the man.

For many years, I had a hunger for carrot cake with cream-cheese frosting. That hunger, however, came to an end when a popular gourmet foods store near my home, Trader Joe's, started selling a delicious carrot cake for only $2.49 a loaf. For about six months straight, I went to Trader Joe's and bought several loaves of carrot cake to snack on. But like with most foods, the novelty soon wore off and now I no longer have carvings for carrot cake whatsoever!

Sometimes we find in our lives that once a hunger is satisfied — whether it be physical or emotional — new and different items will then be needed to keep our appetites going. After a while, we get bored with what we craved, no matter how strong the craving was at first.

When A Man's Interest Fades

Women write to me often with questions and comments around the topic of "what do men really want in a woman?"

Frequently they feel that "men only have one thing on their minds"(sex). However, I also find many complaints about men who seem to lose their desire for sex and physical intimacy with time.

An example of this loss of interest was presented recently by a woman who wrote:

> "I've been dating a great guy for four months. Things moved very quickly at first. We spent every night of the first two months together. Then we agreed to stop the every night thing and went to a four or five days a week pattern. That worked out great for a while, but then all of a sudden he decided that we should stop having sex altogether until he figures out what he wants. We still see each other four to five nights a week and talk a lot but there's no SEX! This man says he cares a lot for me, calls me all the time, and is always asking me to do things with him — including traveling together over the holidays. But he does not want to have sex right now. He told me that he is not sure if he's ready for a committed relationship. I never brought up that issue. Besides, my main concern is what happened to the guy who had the 'hots' for me? I'm so confused and hurt by all of this. Can you tell me what this all means and what I'm supposed to do?"

Evidently, a lot of men these days pursue women too aggressively at first, and then quickly fade away after they get the sex or attention they initially desired so much. On the surface, it looks like men are entirely at fault for this confusing behavior. But even well-meaning, high-quality men can still go through this same kind of progression — aggressive pursuit to gradual withdrawal — despite their deeper wishes for love.

Unleash The "Hottie" Within

Here are some ideas on how a woman can become sexier in the eyes of men. Remember that sexiness is more than skin deep and is largely about being self-confident and expressing yourself tastefully in a feminine way. Check out this list and find some things that you can mix into your personal style. Most of all, keep in mind that it is the "hottie" ingredient that stirs up the initial desire in men and contributes greatly to the high levels of chemistry that are essential for getting a man's elusive commitment.

* Be more open and less close-minded.
* Take good care of your skin with quality sunscreen and moisturizer.
* Find a hairstyle that is currently fashionable and appealing to men.
* Exercise regularly to open up your pores and improve your skin.
* Be proud of your accomplishments and the person you've become.
* Develop a healthy and tasteful sense of humor.
* Maintain your mystique by keeping your personal secrets.
* Get more comfortable with touching and being touched.
* Maintain high standards for clean personal hygiene.
* Become a better kisser and enjoy it more.
* Go to the theater to watch romantic movies when they come out.
* Learn to talk in a more intimate way when the occasion arises.
* Be more sensuous with bubble baths, candles, scented oils, and flowers.
* Have something sexy to wear to bed or sleep in the nude occasionally.
* Learn the important differences between sexiness and sleaziness.
* A sexy body is a healthy body, so exercise, eat right, and be well rested.
* Appreciate your body as it is while you raise your health standards.
* Get your teeth cleaned and whitened so that you can smile more freely.
* Feel more joy/spontaneity and less inhibition with sex.
* Wear some clothes that are soft and sensual.
* Dress fashionably and in ways that compliment your sexiness.
* Listen to music that makes you feel good.
* Learn to look people in the eyes more often.
* Have some clothes that make a man guess what's underneath.
* Buy some clothes for an erotic special occasion.
* Try to develop your ability to flirt with sexy body language.
* Become a better dancer so that you can move with more grace.
* Lighten up on any masculine mannerisms, postures, and gestures.

So what's the root of the problem? What do men really want? And how can a sensible woman keep a good man satisfied but yet hungry for more?

IT'S NOT ALL ABOUT BEING "HOT"

A good friend of mine, fresh from a nasty divorce, became romantically involved with a professional exotic dancer. And yes, she was "hot."

For several months, my buddy Tony was on a fantasy high from the thrills of dating this exciting woman. I'd see him in popular nightclubs showing Cindy off and having a great time with all of the attention that was coming his way. But a few months later, I found out that Tony was back on the prowl again looking for a more suitable love partner to fully invest himself in for the long term.

Tony told me that his brief romance with the exotic dancer was both "the best and worst of times." Apparently, Cindy's unstable and unhealthy lifestyle habits of late hours, drugs, alcohol, and bizarre acquaintances started to drive my friend nuts. The relationship provided a strange mix of passion, excitement, jealousy, fear, and chaos.

As much as Tony liked the "highs," he couldn't handle the ever increasing "lows" of being in that relationship. Besides, my friend confided that the bottom line for him was never being able to "take her home to meet Momma." That meant that Tony couldn't see himself taking the relationship seriously and introducing Cindy to his family.

I'm sure that this exotic dancer was heartbroken with the demise of her relationship with my friend. After all, she was as physically attractive and sexy as a woman could possibly be. But in the end, a relationship that only filled one emotional need, such as excitement, was not enough to sustain my friend's overall desires for his life.

Too much of a good thing can eventually become boring and unfulfilling — especially if it is the only enticing thing that a person has to offer. A big secret to having a successful love relationship is to make sure that the relationship itself offers a combination of both variety and stability.

MEN HAVE MULTIPLE EMOTIONAL HUNGERS

I believe most men equate their love for a woman in terms of their desire for her. They will initially want her attention, affection, companionship, and probably the chance to have sex with her as well. But the danger is that a man can satisfy his initial hunger for a woman and then feel that he's lost his love for her. That's when he starts doubting his love and looks around for other women to stir up his desires.

What makes this more difficult to understand for women is that men also have changing needs. Men may want passion at first, but later want less excitement. Men may also want stability in their relationships, but soon complain after achieving it about becoming bored. Lastly, men may feel loved by a woman and want to connect deeply, but be apprehensive about the responsibilities that go along with investing in a long-term equal partnership.

So what's a sensitive woman to do with the men in her life who have ever-changing desires and hungers that become satisfied so quickly?

SMART MOVE #6: BECOME AN IRRESISTIBLE WOMAN

There are three solutions to this dilemma. One is to tell unenlightened men to take a hike and not even bother with them. Another is to only deal with more appreciative or emotionally mature men who don't have significant issues about commitment. And finally, a woman can develop and offer more facets within herself. In this way, a smart woman can naturally show her most appealing and impressive qualities as the situation dictates.

For example, a woman can offer stability while not being boring. She can be exciting without being chaotic. This same woman can be respected for her accomplishments, admired for her poise, and liked for her warmth and kindness. It all comes down to developing a good personality mix that can flourish in a variety of environments.

To further develop your personality mix, consider these five facets of a woman's persona that should serve you well in getting and keeping a man's attention and love:

✿ **The Hottie.** This is the sexy, feminine part of a woman that makes her desirable to men. Being a "hottie" involves how she looks, moves, and acts. In terms of looks, our popular culture largely defines what makes a woman physically attractive. In addition, a smart woman should aim to be physically fit and have a healthy attitude about her body. A "hottie" acts with confidence, playfulness, sensuality, and mystique. She dresses in a way that accentuates her highlights tastefully. She moves elegantly with attractive and feminine hand gestures, facial expressions, and body postures. Most importantly, the woman who is most largely characterized as a "hottie" is the first one who grabs the attention of men. If you want a man to be really into you from the start, then make a strong impression with your "hottie" element early on. Being a "hottie" isn't everything when it comes to love. But having a "hottie" element in your personality mix makes you more attractive to men and may clearly set you apart from your immediate competition. When the moment is appropriate, don't hesitate to give your dating prospects a good glimpse of your "hottie" ingredient in action.

☙ **The Sweetie.** This is the side of a woman that brings warmth, kindness, sensitivity, and peacefulness to a relationship. The "sweetie" is understanding, supportive, and caring, which are outstanding qualities to have for long-term love relationships. In the short-run, the "sweetie" may be overlooked because of a competing "hottie." The "sweetie" may occasionally hear men say, "I would never want to hurt you" because they may like her more like a sister or close friend than as a lover. But it is the "sweetie" element that men adore and like so it should never be discounted or underappreciated. While a man's physical desires naturally wane, his enjoyment of a true "sweetie" always remains intact. A "hottie" who doesn't have a "sweetie" element within her is a prime candidate for an unfortunate love-hate relationship.

☙ **The Pal.** What good is it for a couple to have common interests, similar values, and mutual attraction, if they can't stand each other? In my years as a professional tour director, I have frequently come across vacationing couples who always seem to get on each other's nerves. I often wonder how miserable their lives have been over all the years. It seems these partners really don't get along, and they treat each other with hostility rather than with the warmth and kindness of a dear friend. True friends are usually patient, kind, supportive, compassionate, and fun to be around. On the other hand, people in difficult relationships will typically treat their partners with an assortment of controlling demands, insensitive remarks, and unfair judgments. A strong "pal" side of a woman allows her to be a great companion who can easily get along with a man's friends and family. She naturally becomes a part of his social lifestyle. She is someone that he can enjoy taking anywhere, under most any circumstance, regardless of whom else is there. The woman who has a strong "Pal" element can expect to spend more time with a man, and she will have a better chance of expanding their relationship into a more full-time true love partnership.

☙ **The Prize.** Men often value a woman based partly on what other men think. As silly as it might sound, this behavior is based on a psychological element identified as "social proof" by Dr. Robert B. Cialdini in the book, *Influence: The New Psychology of Modern Persuasion.* The principle behind "social proof" is that we unconsciously will feel and do the same as others around us. In the case of "The Prize," a woman who is desired by other men will have a higher perceived value. If a woman isn't desired by others, that naturally makes a man wonder if there might be something wrong with her as a potential love partner. When a woman is highly "prized," then a man will recognize his window of opportunity with her. He'll know that if he doesn't act quickly, he probably won't get a chance with her again. This man's fear is that she will be won over by the next guy who tries to get her attention. The fear of a lost opportunity causes men to pursue quicker and harder with a woman who is in demand.

🌀 **The Person.** This part of a woman is respected for her accomplishments, talents, knowledge, expertise, and strength of character. A sensitive man is in awe of any woman who can consistently demonstrate her strengths as an overall responsible, mature, trustworthy, and loving human-being. This kind of respect becomes a vital ingredient to making any love relationship work in the long term, whether it's a social, professional, or romantic relationship. When a woman enters the dating world without a strong "Person" element, she will likely come across men who treat her like a doormat. They will be inclined to ignore the loving individual that she truly is inside.

By integrating these five aspects into your personality mix, you will become an irresistible love partner that men will want to have in their lives. This is the only kind of woman who will have the impact, versatility, dimension, depth, and endurance to keep a man's ever-changing desires satisfied over the long haul.

WHAT TO DO NOW

Take a moment and give yourself a grade (A = excellent, B = above average, C = average, D = below average, F = very weak) for each of the five facets mentioned previously. Next, based on the grades you've given yourself, figure out what is the strongest and weakest part of your dating personality.

If, for example, the strongest ingredient of your personality is "The Sweetie," make sure that you let your warmth and kindness shine in the beginning of your next dating experience. Notice the effect that you have on other people when you go immediately towards your strength.

Now think of someone you know who is strong in an area where you are weaker. Hang out with that person and start noticing how they think and what they do in order to let that part of them shine. With a commitment to constant improvement, you can elevate your weaker facets until they reach a point where they also shine in the jewel of your personality.

The key here is to identify and evaluate the strengths and weaknesses of your dating persona. Then commit to improving yourself through focus and practice. That way, you can become at least a "B" in every facet for the benefit of your own self-confidence and the long-term attention of men.

Note that a certain man may find one or more particular facets of your personality more appealing than others. As your relationship develops, be aware of keeping those facets especially strong, while maintaining a balance of the others for your satisfaction and his.

THE BOTTOM LINE

Dating sucks when you either can't attract a good man or are unable to keep men interested in you very long. But dating rocks when your appeal is powerful enough to attract a wide choice of high-quality suitors. Then your varied personality mix will be even more richly appreciated as your love relationship develops over time.

Seven

Losing Candidates

DATING SUCKS WHEN YOU CHOOSE THE WRONG MEN

"A woman has got to love a bad man
once or twice in her life to be thankful
for a good one."

Marjorie Kinnan Rawlings
Author of *The Yearling* (1938)

can•di•date: 1. a person who seeks or is nominated for an office, prize, or honor. 2. in the context of dating, a prospective partner who is considered a good match. 3. a critical choice that a woman makes in her search for true love.

An honest male perspective: Love won't work if you select the wrong partner. There is a lot more to consider than just mutual attraction when it comes to determining whether another person is suited for you over the long term. Before you get emotionally involved, be sure to evaluate your prospective love-partner based on compatibility, emotional maturity, romantic chemistry, and growth. Otherwise, you'll be faced with a relationship that's not going to work for either of you.

Every four years, the two major political parties go through a process of nominating a candidate for the office of President of the United States. During 2004, the Democrats held primaries throughout the country and Senator John Kerry of Massachusetts came out ahead of his party's other candidates. His Democratic rivals included Congressman Dennis Kucinich, Governor Howard Dean, General Wesley Clark, Reverend Al Sharpton, and Senators Joe Lieberman and John Edwards.

With the massive expenses in time, energy, and money, the wisest choice for each political party is to back the candidate who possesses the highest chance of winning in the November national elections.

Similarly, a smart woman wants to back a winner and not a sure loser if she wants to have the best chance of succeeding at love. While there are many finer variables for picking a potential winner for each individual situation, there are definite traits of men who will most likely end up being a waste of a woman's precious resources. These traits are the ones you should look out for to ensure that you won't waste time in someone who isn't a winner.

Separate The Winners From The Losers

With the convenience and popularity of online dating, some women are meeting a larger number of seemingly eligible men than ever before. Yet it doesn't take much for a man to write an appealing personal profile and be able to carry on a friendly online conversation. A smart woman realizes that with so little to go on, it's difficult to determine with any certainty whether a man she meets on the Internet is going to be a winner or a loser in her search for true love.

On a similar note, a woman wrote to me recently expressing her concern about evaluating the man she was dating:

> "What does it mean when a guy says he likes you, but that he's not feeling the spark? The guy that I've been seeing for several months told me once in the beginning that we had good chemistry, but now he says this junk. What gives with this guy? Doesn't a man either like you or not like you?"

One of the most common lines of questions that a woman will send me is basically about whether a man that she meets is interested in her or not. While gauging a man's interest is a primary task, I always remind women that it is equally important to determine if the man is right *for her.*

By evaluating whether or not the man in question has sincere interest, plus whether or not he is a good relationship match, a woman is more likely to avoid falling in love with the wrong man. Thus she may ultimately prevent relationship failure.

DON'T COUNT ON PEOPLE CHANGING — ESPECIALLY MEN!

Avoiding losing candidates for love is not always an easy thing to do. Since most people are so hopeful for love but meet only a small number of potential sweethearts, they tend to make the most of any romantic opportunity that comes their way.

Several years ago, I was introduced to a lovely young woman who was fourteen years my junior. I remember getting word of her telling a friend that "Steve is neat guy who has a lot to offer," which was certainly true compared to the guys she was dating at the time. But it was only during our first month of dating that she continued to see me in the best light — as being mature, easygoing, and financially stable. During this "honeymoon" dating period, it seemed like I was a man who could do no wrong.

During the second month of our dating relationship, this young woman saw me in a completely different way. My perceived "maturity" transformed into my being viewed as "acting like her father." What was earlier described as "easygoing" became "being lazy, old, and tired." And what was described as "financially stable" became being "frugal" or "obsessed with money."

Looking back now, I can see how differences in ages, interests, and relationship goals made me a losing candidate for this particular woman. As a result of these dividing issues, it was no surprise that our dating relationship ended after a brief two-month audition.

Smart Move #7: Avoid Losing Love Candidates

It's important to remind yourself that people rarely change. Therefore, it is much wiser to mainly evaluate a new love interest based on how they are *right now* — not predominantly on their potential. The nature of romance makes it easy to get caught up in a passionate moment without regard for longer-term issues like compatibility and growth. But smart women are careful to evaluate things early in the game and before getting emotionally involved. That way, a woman can avoid staying too long with the wrong kind of man.

> "The only time a woman really succeeds
> in changing a man is when he's a baby."
> Natalie Wood
> American actress (1938-1981)

Here are ways that any woman can realize she's dating a man who is a losing candidate for her love life:

⌘ **Steer clear of men with destructive personal habits.** If a prospective man has a chronic drug, alcohol, or gambling habit, then it would be prudent to avoid getting romantically involved with him. Destructive habits control people's lives and the lives of those around them. Many women have learned painful lessons by wasting their time, energy, and emotions on these poor love candidates.

⌘ **Avoid men with serious character flaws.** Character is the foundation of every individual. It is the result of hundreds of choices that a person has made which gradually molded them into the kind of person they are today. Many women today are faced with increasing numbers of men whose character flaws create a very unstable foundation for love. Character is something that takes time to develop and is solely the responsibility of each individual. Therefore, a smart woman would be better off steering clear of men with major character flaws rather than getting involved and trying to change them.

☙ **Pass on men who lack any kind of ambition**. To many women, this may not seem as severe as the other traits to avoid. But just the same, a woman quickly tires of a man who lacks the ambition to maximize his potential. This trait often leads to a lack of financial resources which is a major cause of stress in marriages. A smart woman needs to differentiate between a man who is at peace with himself and one that is simply lazy and unmotivated. The latter is the kind of man who starts to wear on a woman in an unpleasant way over time.

☙ **Don't date men who don't turn you on**. There is no substitute for high levels of chemistry or physical attraction as part of the mix of what a relationship offers. If this chemistry doesn't come naturally after a reasonable period of time, then it is best to avoid getting more deeply involved. Otherwise, you'll get stuck in a passionless relationship and this is not healthy or fulfilling for either partner.

☙ **Say "No!" to men who are mean-spirited**. Women are often confused by a man who shows kindness in one moment and hostility the next. It's common for women to focus on the good behavior in the beginning and ignore the negative things until after she's become emotionally attached. When you associate with a man who is mean-spirited, it's only a matter of time before his general bitterness eventually gets redirected towards you.

☞ **Evaluate men by the crowd they run with regularly.** This is a tough thing for many women to do. For some reason, a woman wants to believe that her man is a lot different than his peers. This goes against the more likely scenario that he is only showing you the sides that would appeal to you. In reality, he is most likely to be a lot more like those men he has as friends and associates. Consider this rather than solely evaluating the version of himself that he's trying to sell you on.

☞ **Avoid men who naturally clash with your personality.** Some people just don't seem to get along very well. Instead of complementing each other with their mutual support, two people can clash on simple day-to-day issues, and bring out the worst in each other. If you find yourself in one of these difficult relationships, it is much better to, at best, keep things limited. Don't make the mistake of trying to create an expanded relationship by, for example, marrying a man who causes you emotional upsets on a consistent basis.

☞ **Beware of major lifestyle mismatches.** How we choose to live our lives is expressed in the clothes we wear, the music we play, the things we buy, the foods we love to eat, the words we speak, the dreams we hold dear, the friends we choose, and the activities we enjoy in our free time. If we want to share a life with someone, it makes more sense to find a partner who matches our lifestyle habits rather than one who doesn't. People with mismatching lifestyles may add color and variety to our lives, but usually they are best suited for a more limited relationship or friendship.

𑁉 **Recognize potential values conflicts immediately.** Values — such as courage, love, integrity, and family — are the ideals that we hold in the highest regard. When two people don't share the same values, then deep upsets naturally occur in the relationship. For example, I've heard from married women who complain about husbands who get drunk with their buddies instead of doing more responsible things for the marriage. Such a value conflict between responsibility and fun would need to be discussed and resolved before resentment sets in. As a woman in search of a new partner, it makes sense for you to avoid men who clearly don't have the same values as you do. Values, which are really deep-rooted priorities, are not likely to change easily without the aid of significant emotional events.

𑁉 **Spot a man with contrary relationship goals.** It's easy to be fooled by the man who insists that he loves kids, but only has the opportunity to show this trait when the children belong to someone else. A smart woman needs to distinguish between a man who only talks about getting married and having a family and the man who would actually embrace the responsibility of following through. Of course, other men say directly that they have no intention of starting a family and only express the desire to concentrate on their other personal goals. A woman may be fooled into thinking that such a man will change in time, but later discover that his original relationship goals were deeply ingrained. A smart woman will carefully gauge a man's priorities in life so that she is properly aligned with him. Men who only want a limited kind of relationship are only good for women who want the same thing. This is another example of where expecting other people to change is almost always a long-shot proposition.

By making a thorough examination of dating candidates, a smart woman can back the man who has the best chances of becoming a winner in her love life. This process involves first weeding out the obvious losers and then concentrating on the potential winners.

WHAT TO DO NOW

Write down an example of each type of man described in the previous section. Your example could be someone you've dated or known as an acquaintance, someone that one of your girlfriends has been associated with, or even a character that you're familiar with from politics, sports, music, television, or movies.

The important thing is for you to have a clear image of what a losing candidate looks like as soon as possible. That way, you can make an instant connection to one of the profiles if a man warns you with obvious clues about himself in the early stages of dating.

THE BOTTOM LINE

Dating sucks when you get involved romantically with the wrong man. But dating rocks when there's a healthy love relationship brewing between two people with high levels of mutual attraction, compatibility, and emotional maturity. It's great when you're truly good for each other!

Eight

Bad Odds

DATING SUCKS WHEN YOU'RE IN A POOR LOVE SITUATION

"Whenever I date a guy, I think,
is this the man I want my children
to spend their weekends with?"

Rita Rudner
American stand-up comedian

bad odds: 1. when the likelihood of failure occurring as expressed in a ratio is much greater than the likelihood of success. 2. in the context of dating, when the prospects for true love are not good because of the poor circumstances surrounding your relationship. 3. what smart women learn to recognize quickly and avoid in their love lives.

An honest male perspective: Don't act foolishly by expecting love longshots to win! When you are faced with a low-percentage romantic situation, realize that the most likely outcome is failure. The smart move is to only get involved when the love situation is favorable.

The signs of booming times in the gambling industry have been everywhere. Casinos are popping up all over America, a major corporate merger between MGM Grand Hotels and Mandalay Bay Resorts dominated the front page of *The Wall Street Journal,* and prime-time network television shows such as *C.S.I., Las Vegas,* and *The Casino* have been shot on location in Nevada showcasing a gambling subculture.

This gambling mania seems to overlook the fundamental fact that casinos thrive on millions of people losing their money in games of chance. In these games, the odds are bad for the player, but good for the casino. As an old gambling adage so wisely points out, "The best way to win a small fortune in Las Vegas is to start with a big fortune."

In a similar way, many people take foolish chances in their love lives. And when the odds of succeeding with a new relationship are bad, you end up wasting your precious time, energy, and emotions on losing romance propositions.

WHEN LOVE DOESN'T WORK

Each week, I receive at least one message from a woman who is deeply involved in a love situation where the odds of succeeding are very low. Here's an example:

> "My so-called boyfriend of almost a year has another girlfriend, someone that he lives with. For the past three months, he's been saying that he loves me. This man said that he wants to provide for me, and he claimed he was getting his act together so that he could move out and end his other relationship. But we had a big fight last night about his current living situation. Now he says he is going to distance himself from me. I think that maybe his girlfriend is putting the screws to him. Or have I just been playing the fool all this time? What do you think I should I do?"

I usually respond to these kinds of stories by telling the woman that at least three things are needed to make any relationship work: *the right man, the right woman, and the right situation.* The most confusing scenario is when you put the right man and the right woman together in the wrong situation. Inevitably, the wrong situation presents a consistent long-term obstacle that many romances can't seem to overcome, even when it feels good initially.

WHEN I LOST OUT TO BAD ODDS

Years ago, a love relationship provided a painful lesson for me. I was involved with a woman who I believed at the time to be "the love of my life." Earlier in the book I mentioned this passionate romance, which started on a beautiful secluded beach in the Bahamas. Our relationship ended after two years when the woman fell for a more suitable man who she eventually married.

Many years later, I had a chance to talk to her and she shared a deep, dark secret with me. She said that our relationship was doomed from the beginning because her father didn't approve of my Japanese-American heritage. This was something that she felt too ashamed of to discuss with me back then.

In addition, our relationship was a long-distance romance which meant she would have had to eventually relocate. It was far more convenient for this woman to choose her current husband who resided nearby instead of me.

Looking back at this situation, I now know the reason that I lost out with this woman was not because I wasn't the right kind of man. And it wasn't that she was the wrong kind of woman for me. It was a simple case of the odds of the situation not being in our favor.

SMART MOVE #8: AVOID LOW-PERCENTAGE LOVE SITUATIONS

Adversity tests the strength of your love with another person. The more difficult the situation, the harder it is to make love work. This doesn't necessarily mean that a low-percentage situation won't work out. Many couples have overcome tremendous obstacles and gone on to enjoy lasting love-relationships. But a romance based almost exclusively on superficial things such as physical attraction, for example, will quickly be exposed for what it is when faced with a long-term challenging situation.

To help you assess your love situation more accurately, here are some obstacles that may hurt your chances for finding success at lasting true-love:

⊛ **Stay clear of married and almost married men.** Men who are married, separated, engaged, or already involved in some other kind of committed relationship make poor candidates for true love. These types of men are notorious for stringing along innocent women, and rarely do they make the decision to move away from the current situation as promised. Don't fall into the trap of being the "spice" in a man's love life. Instead, find a situation where you will be the "main course." Make sure that a man makes a clean break from his previous relationship before you make yourself vulnerable.

⊛ **Avoid men with excessive family problems.** Initially, a man may hide the fact that there are problems with his immediate family. His troublesome relatives (parents, children, etc.) will often take priority over any new romantic interests that may appear only short-term to him. Also realize that some family problems can be closely linked to hidden financial strains.

⊛ **Beware of the geographically undesirable.** When two people live a long way from each other, it limits their actual time together or makes getting together a major hassle. If an emotional attachment takes hold and transforms itself into a long-distance romance, eventually a major relocation will be required or dreams will be broken. Relocating for someone is risky business, and shattered

"...but enough about me."

dreams bring heartache. So carefully consider any involvement with a man who lives in a different part of the country, continent, or world.

🕭 **Be wary of romances with traveling men.** A lot of innocent women get involved with men who are on a trip for business or pleasure. For some of these men, there is a challenge to see if they can score while traveling regardless of their relationship at home. As a recent commercial about Las Vegas suggests, "What happens in Las Vegas *stays* in Las Vegas." For some men, whatever they do while on a trip is all right as long as they don't intentionally try to hurt another person and nobody back home finds out. Single men may view travel time as an opportunity to have sex "without strings" or a way to get quick sex despite having STDs. Steer clear of these men, or proceed cautiously.

🕭 **Look out for large age differences.** While this obstacle may not apply so much to celebrity love relationships, it is a more common problem for the average person. Large age-differences translate into being in different stages in life, and make it hard to relate well to each other over time. Often, the younger partner starts to blossom while the older partner tends to feel uncomfortable about this change. For some rare couples, this kind of change ends the original dynamics of the relationship, but they manage to reach a new balance of power and go on to lovingly grow together.

🕭 **Don't discount religion, race, and ethnic issues.** If marriage and starting a family are part of your future plans, then religion, race, and ethnic issues may appear prominently in a romantic relationship. For some recently matched individuals with these kinds of strong cultural ties, such issues may be too much of an obstacle to moving forward in a dating relationship towards marriage.

🐬 **Beware of class distinctions.** Sometimes economic and social differences can also take their toll on a new love relationship. There is a certain level of difference that most people can accommodate. However, if there are large and clear differences here, a rift may begin to take hold and widen. Of course, in movies like *Pretty Woman*, people of different classes may spark interesting romances that are successful. Still, in real life, social and economic differences have a largely negative influence on long-term success with love.

🐬 **Take careful note of major scheduling conflicts.** Sometimes I hear women complain that the man they are dating is always working. Maybe he owns his own business and works an 80 to 90 hour work-week. This type of man does not leave much room in his schedule for a full-time love relationship. Another common situation is when the man works the graveyard shift (midnight to 8 A.M.) and the woman works a typical eight-to-five shift. If you're a woman who wants to spend a lot of time with your man, then these kinds of love situations are going to be difficult and stressful for you.

🐬 **Watch out for unfair competition.** Sometimes a woman will have to compete with an almost perfect mother, an adorable sister, a gorgeous ex-girlfriend, or a loyal ex-wife for a man's affection. While this special person may not even be directly related to his current love life, the comparisons of her personal strengths may be matched up unfairly against any new woman who comes along.

Be on the lookout for these obvious clues that a relationship most likely won't work out. Don't be fooled by your short-term emotions when the long-term facts point in the opposite direction. The decision to pass when the odds are bad is much less painful to do right away than after two people have become emotionally involved.

WHAT TO DO NOW

Think back to a relationship in your past and see if any of the "bad odds" situations I've mentioned contributed to its eventual downfall. If you have an extensive dating history, can you see any kind of pattern or tendency on your part?

Take out a piece of paper and write down a checklist of the situations that you do want to have in your present or upcoming relationship. The importance of this exercise is to develop a quick recognition of the circumstances around your love life. That way, you can take more decisive actions when the stakes are small.

The best strategy is to save your resources for love situations that look good from the start. This is as opposed to fighting an uphill battle against a relationship that only has a small chance of ever working out.

THE BOTTOM LINE

Dating sucks when you're stuck in a low-percentage love situation where the prospects of advancing to a happy marriage do not seem likely. But dating rocks when a smart woman learns to recognize poor love-situations quickly and moves on to the prospects for love that are more favorable.

Nine

People Skills

DATING ROCKS WHEN YOU
GET ALONG WELL WITH OTHERS

"The average man is more interested
in a woman who is interested in him
than in a woman – any woman –
with beautiful legs."

Marlene Dietrich
German-born American Actress (1901-1992)

peo•ple skills: 1. the ability to get along well with others. 2. the refined study and use of successful human-relations principles. 3. what every woman needs to develop, use, and maintain in order to maximize her social opportunities.

An honest male perspective: Attracting, getting, and maintaining long-lasting love requires both partners to practice sound human-relations skills. When the going gets rough, smart people remain patient, kind, compassionate and, most of all, flexible in their approach to one another. Remember the Golden Rule which reads: "Do unto others as you would have others do unto you." In other words, treat others as you want to be treated. If you don't, poor people skills will make you an undesirable person to spend time with.

A few years ago, the *National Enquirer* ran a story with the headline: "Angry Tori Spelling Snubs *90210* Reunion because Shannen Will Be There!" Evidently Tori Spelling, a prominent cast member of the hit 1990's teenage drama *Beverly Hills, 90210,* was upset that her supposed bitter rival, Shannen Doherty, was invited back to take part in the show's 10th-year reunion TV special program.

According to the tabloids, Ms. Doherty's alleged temper-tantrums and unprofessional conduct on the *Beverly Hills, 90210* set infuriated other cast members enough to demand that she get fired from the show. These same kinds of allegations have continued to plague Ms. Doherty throughout the rest of her professional career.

One might guess that Shannen Doherty's apparent lack of "people skills" may also have contributed a small part to her two brief marriages. Despite an abundance of significant positive attributes — such as fame, charisma, wealth, talent, youth, and strikingly good looks — an otherwise desirable woman like Shannen Doherty can still find difficulty making a long-term love relationship work.

Whether you're a famous television celebrity or an average person, the ability to get along well with others is important to maintaining any kind of interpersonal relationship. And when it comes to being desired as a romantic candidate, remember that no sensible man wants to spend very much time with a woman whose company is unpleasant.

WHEN REALITY SHOWS UP IN YOUR RELATIONSHIPS

I often receive personal messages from concerned women when the so-called honeymoon period of their relationship ends and the first signs of conflict begin to surface. It's not unusual for such arguments to trigger doubts about their future with that particular man.

Ideally we would all like things in our love-life to stay tranquil forever. However, the reality is that some form of conflict is inevitable. It is how well we handle this conflict that largely determines whether we will enjoy an expanded love-relationship, a limited one, or none at all.

Here is an example of not using people-skills effectively:

> "My boyfriend told me that I am difficult to be
> with because I am so stubborn. Of course, he
> always says this in jest. Does a man not like it
> when a woman is a good debater and can, for the

most part, prove her point and be right? I am the type where if I have an opinion, I will say it no matter what. And when I'm challenged, I prefer to take the offensive, rather than remain on the defensive. He says that he fell in love with my mind, so I keep on being stubborn when we argue. Could this be a problem for us now?"

Many people constantly get into everyday conflict with others. Women who don't get along with her boyfriend's friends or family members may find that the built-up resentment eventually destroys the relationship with their man. Therefore, developing and maintaining a good set of practical "people skills" will well serve any woman in her quest for the long-lasting love that she desires.

WINNING FRIENDS AND INFLUENCING PEOPLE

Years ago, I taught the Dale Carnegie Course on improved human-relations and effective public-speaking. The coursework was based on Mr. Carnegie's perennial worldwide bestseller, *How to Win Friends and Influence People.*

I taught Mr. Carnegie's principles to a lot of middle managers who were in need of this basic training. Every Wednesday night for fifteen weeks, each class member was assigned to make a two-minute speech. These speeches were based on how they had successfully applied one of the Dale Carnegie human-relations principles in their workplace or personal lives.

The program set two basic goals for the students. One was that by the end of 15 weeks, they would each gain the self-confidence to stand up and speak effectively. Second, and just as important, they'd have a long list of experiences of successfully applying "people skills" to the relationships in their personal lives and at work.

Based on the testimony of each class member on the final day of the Dale Carnegie Course, I can safely say that the consistent use of proven human-relations principles can work successfully for any person and in every relationship situations including love.

SMART MOVE #9: MASTER YOUR PEOPLE SKILLS

In order to get along well with others, you must realize that one of the main things all people want is to feel important. In addition, when you realize that there is always something you can learn from someone else, it is much easier to appreciate them. How well you appreciate and value other people will largely determine how well you get along with them, regardless of the technique that you apply.

Here are some simple ways to fine-tune your ability to get along well with other people and improve your human-relations skills for a better love life:

⊛ **Start off by being friendly and cheerful.** Remember that first impressions are formed during the initial few seconds of an interaction. That's why it's always a safe policy to start off by putting your best foot forward. A good way to accomplish this is to be friendly and cheerful. A warm smile also communicates this feeling in a natural way. People frequently make the mistake of trying too hard to impress someone in the beginning. However usually the other person just wants is to feel comfortable and have an

"Oh, the comfort –
the inexpressible comfort
of feeling *safe* with a person –
having neither to weigh
thoughts nor measure words,
but pouring them all right
out, just as they are, chaff
and grain together; certain
that a faithful hand will take
and sift them, keep what is
worth keeping, and then
with the breath of human
kindness blow the rest away."

Dinah Maria Mulock Craik
English novelist and poet (1826-1887)

enjoyable experience. If you do not make a good impression, you may not get a chance to make a second one.

🙂 **Relax and be natural.** Another helpful technique to master is having an opening greeting in mind to use. Keep it simple and natural such as "Hi, how are you doing?" Rather than dumping a clever line on another person, it's far better to be relaxed and communicate in a natural manner. This puts the other person at ease.

🙂 **Don't criticize or complain.** In my work as a tour director, I've had my fill of people who criticize and complain about almost anything. While they may have legitimate reasons for doing this, the end result is that these people enjoy their vacations less and tend to bring other travelers down. If these types of people could only rid themselves of the need to feel more important by making such comments, then they would open up their lives to more social opportunities and better-quality relationships with others. Unfortunately, habitual complainers are the last ones to find out how many love-chances passed them by because of their negative nature. By not being negative, you not only open yourself up to additional possibilities, you will actually allow yourself to enjoy them more, too.

🙂 **Connect on the same level.** Be aware that most communication between people is done on an unconscious level. A well-documented study by Dr. Albert Mehrabian at the University of California, Los Angeles, showed that non-verbal communication — including facial, eye, and body movements — account for 55% of all communication. According to this research, only 7% of communication

Unconscious Rapport Skills

For seven years, I learned and applied communication techniques working as a personal development trainer for peak performance expert Tony Robbins' Mastery University seminars.

What I've surmised is that some unconscious communication techniques are worth trying to master because they are easy and natural to do. However, other methods are extremely difficult and make a novice practitioner come across as being either strange or manipulative.

Based on my experience both in dating and communication, here are some simple things to do and avoid when you're trying to connect on the same level with people that you meet in a social situation. (Note: Some of the methods below can be used in a more complex way, and they are mostly mentioned for the benefit of those already familiar with studies in unconscious communication patterns.)

* Get yourself comfortable first and foremost.
* Match your voice volume and talking speed with the other person.
* Match their keywords, phrases, jargon, and slang words.
* Find the comfort level for the amount of eye contact.
* Find the comfort level for body closeness or amount of space.
* Find the comfortable time-balance between talking and listening.
* Don't break their pattern with a strange or loud laugh.
* Don't break their pattern with radical hand-gestures.
* Don't break their pattern with overly dramatic facial expressions.
* Don't overuse annoying pet phrases like "Been there, done that."
* Don't attempt to interpret confusing eye-movement patterns.
* Don't try to match voice textures (nasal tones, strong accents).
* Don't try to persuade with embedded commands or meanings.
* Use tag questions like "You like me, don't you?" very sparingly.
* Don't try using physical anchoring (touching) techniques.
* Don't try to match or mirror back breathing patterns.
* Don't overdo mimicking body postures or hand gestures.
* Don't overuse questions in an effort to redirect their focus.

The Bottom Line

Master the easy and natural ways of building rapport and spend the majority of your focus on being a more likeable, warm, and receptive person. That way, the proper credit will go directly to the person you truly are, instead of to a set of manipulative persuasion tricks. Trust that true bonding between people is spiritual and human in nature.

comes from the actual words we use and 38% of our communication consists of simple voice inflections. In order to connect on the same level, a smart communicator will match another person's basic voice-traits (volume and speed) and non-vocal patterns (hand gestures, amount of eye contact, and basic facial expressions). For more insights on effective nonverbal communication, please refer to the opposite page.

ⓥ **Don't constantly tell other people they are wrong.** We waste a lot of energy trying to be right. In the meantime, we inadvertently make other people feel wrong. What's funny is that we often have good intentions when telling someone they are wrong. As concerned friends, we don't want people we care about to go down the wrong path toward unhappiness, failure, or disappointment. But corrective remarks often result in defensiveness from the other person. So when the stakes are small, be sure to let some harmless comments or behavior go by unchallenged. This allows others to recognize that you approve and accept them as they are. And then be very selective about the things you do address.

ⓥ **Avoid gossip.** Many people have a natural urge to stick their noses into other people's business. For some, this is a kind of entertainment that focuses on the faults of others rather than their strengths. The danger with gossip is that it is filled with speculation, questions people's motives, and is usually designed to criticize or belittle others. Most gossip involves friends, co-workers, or neighbors, so the words of the one who gossips often get back to the accused. People start to wonder what is said about them when they aren't around. If you are viewed as a gossip, people will consider you untrustworthy. The safe strategy is to mind your own business. Also, simply by listening to gossip, you encourage it.

۞ Give sincere person-centered compliments. While teaching the Dale Carnegie Course, I had to have a variety of uniquely positive things to say about my students after their speeches. I would usually look for something that I liked, admired, trusted, or respected about that person. Later, in the dating arena, I found that making an effort to find the less obvious and more personal compliment was a sign that I truly valued the woman at a deeper level. For example, instead of telling a beautiful woman that she was pretty, I would listen intently and say that I enjoyed her sense of humor or respected her opinion about something. That always seemed to score bigger points with my dates and it made me stand out among the other men the woman knew.

۞ Win arguments by avoiding the unnecessary ones! A lot of wasted energy is spent trying to win arguments rather than letting the other person express his or her ideas freely. Sometimes you must remind yourself that many battles aren't worth fighting. It's better to save your ability to discuss differences for the issues that are really important in your relationships. If you feel you could be better at dealing with relationship conflicts, read *I'm Right. You're Wrong. Now What?: How to Break Through Any Relationship Stalemate Without Fighting, Folding or Fleeing* by JacLynn Morris, M.Ed. and Paul L. Fair, Ph.D.

Improving your human-relation skills may require breaking some old patterns and habits. However, excelling in your people skills is an attractive quality that allows the chance for love to flourish. Your ability to get along with a wide variety of people under different sets of circumstances goes a long way toward making sure that your love relationship is an expanded, growing one — not a limited dying one.

WHAT TO DO NOW

Take a moment now and think of someone you can identify as in need of improved people-skills. Maybe it's a negative co-worker, a miserable friend who brings you down, or even a dearly loved relative who can't seem to get along with people for very long. With each example, identify a solution to their problem from the key points that you learned here.

Now take a closer look at yourself. In what simple way can you improve your people-skills with those that you interact with each day? Resolve to focus on each one of the key points mentioned in this chapter so that you can have a successful experience applying human-relations principles in your own life. Before long, you will begin to realize that getting along better with others is a simple skill that any person can develop. It just requires some informed conscious effort.

THE BOTTOM LINE

Dating sucks when you don't get along well with others and are a pain to be around for very long. But dating rocks when people enjoy your company and deeply value their association with you under all kinds of social circumstances.

Ten

Small Talk

DATING ROCKS WHEN MEN TUNE IN TO HEAR YOU SPEAK

"Good conversation is what makes us interesting. Why be bored and why be boring when you don't have to be either?"

Edwin Newman
Award-winning television commentator

small talk: 1. a casual verbal exchange that is mainly meant to just be enjoyable for all parties involved. 2. speaking in an interesting way about the everyday things that occur in a person's life. 3. what smart women master in order to get men to pay attention and partake in lively conversations.

An honest male perspective: Men listen attentively to the radio shows they like best as well as to the favorite people in their real lives. If you want to get and keep a man's attention, make sure you take up the slack in your small talk. Otherwise, your love prospects may start tuning out early and not give you a fair chance to shine.

For 17 months, NBC's hit television reality show, *Last Comic Standing*, featured a nationwide talent search for the best amateur and professional comedians. In the first two series of competitions, a detailed selection process narrowed the field down to 10 finalists who then lived together in a house in the Hollywood Hills. The third and last competition focused on pure stand-up, with no footage of comedians sharing living space. The prizes for the third winner included a one-hour special appearance on *Comedy Central* and $250,000, along with that round's title as the "Last Comic Standing."

The show offered viewers a chance to see a wide variety of stand-up comics who performed in short segments. While all of the final contestants were effective comedians to some degree, the final episodes of the show clearly demonstrated the wide differences in communication mastery between those who advance and those who go home.

During the first season of *Last Comic Standing,* the winner was a young Vietnamese-American man named Dat Phan. Dat masterfully grabbed the audience's attention and entertained them with unique, tasteful humor that left a lasting favorable impression. Among his awards from *Last Comic Standing* were a spot on the *Tonight Show with Jay Leno* and a *Comedy Central* special.

Dat Phan has gone on to appear at nightclubs in cities across the country, including Las Vegas, New Orleans, San Diego, and San Francisco. His current schedule is hectic and amazing.

Like a winning comedian, a woman who aspires to be effective at small talk with men must be able to grab a man's attention quickly, communicate or entertain tastefully, and leave a favorable impression. That way, a man will be more likely to stay tuned in instead of tuned out to her in their conversations. Once a woman acquires the art of small talk, she will have a skill set that will help her advance to higher levels of commitment in the relationship.

EXPECT MEN TO HAVE SHORT ATTENTION SPANS

Many women have complained to me over the years about the men in their love life who either don't listen very well or choose not to engage in extended conversation. Often these women mistakenly believed that this was the result of a problem in the man. The women assumed that he didn't communicate well, and they never considered the effect that they might be having on the interaction.

"My sister has a big mouth and likes to ramble on all the time. She also curses like a sailor, and is quite frankly an overall disagreeable and nasty person. I'm certain that the way she talks and her foul language has scared off lots of men. The sad thing is that she is also pretty cute and has a wonderful romantic side to her, but she hasn't got a clue as to her obvious bad side and why the men she meets don't ever call her. What can I do to help her?"

An example of how poor speaking habits can ruin a woman's chances for love

As in dancing where it "takes two to tango," two people are required to keep conversations flowing. While it may be easy for a woman to talk freely with her female friends, it takes some refined adjustments in order to have an equally positive experience when conversing with a man. In order to relate well with the opposite sex, the man and woman need to bridge a looming possible communication gap. This can be accomplished by becoming more receptive to each other's differences in perceptions and priorities.

> "The conversation of two people remembering, if the memory is enjoyable to both, rocks on like music or lovemaking. There is a rhythm and a predictability to it that each anticipates and relishes."
>
> Jessamyn West
> Author of *The State of Stony Lonesome* (1984)

So in order to get a man to listen and willingly engage in lively conversation, a smart woman needs to know how to talk to a man in a way that will be appealing to him. While all men are certainly not the same, there are definite ways to approach this whether you're faced with a shy, tongue-tied man or a guy who is an outspoken conversationalist.

LESSONS FROM DOING OVER 200 RADIO INTERVIEWS

I promoted my first book, *Men Are Like Fish*, by doing phone-in interviews on radio stations across the U.S. and Canada. My interviews ranged anywhere from five minutes to two hours on mostly fast-paced morning drive-time radio shows. On these kinds of shows, a guest needs to get to the point quickly, be entertaining, and engage the host in lively

119

dialogue in order to be effective. The content of my book was not nearly as important to the show producers as their need for me to be an interesting guest. If I failed to connect well with the hosts and their audience, I was usually cut off the air immediately.

I remember doing an interview for a rock station in Florida whose target listening audience was 20-year-old men. While being friendly to me off the air, the two "shock jocks" attacked me for writing a sissy women's book as soon as the live interview began. While I usually don't like to talk about dating in a negative way, I thought that I'd cater my talk to this particular audience by discussing all the sneaky things that men do to fool innocent women in their quest for sex and romance. The interview went especially well. As a result, I was asked to appear on the show two more times.

With the high cost of airtime, a show producer couldn't afford to have a guest who made their audience want to tune out by not connecting quickly and/or relating well.

SMART MOVE #10: GET MEN TUNED IN TO YOU

Here are some helpful pointers on how to get men to listen more attentively to you and draw them into lively conversations:

☞ **Get to the point quickly.** Being brief allows the other person a chance to talk. If what you have to say requires a lot of verbiage, make sure that you get to the point as quickly as possible. Skip all of the unnecessary details. Otherwise you run the risk of losing a man's interest early in the conversation. Your women friends may be eager to share the burden of your emotional load, but don't expect men to do the same. More than likely, a man will listen long enough to get the gist of the problem and then he'll spend the rest of the time either trying to figure out a solution or developing a rational analysis of your story.

☺ **Don't dwell too long on the negatives.** Watching the nightly news or reading the morning newspaper exposes you to an abundance of negativity. It almost seems that the news of the world is meant to satisfy pessimists. You may have every excuse to talk extensively about what's wrong in the world, but keep in mind that too much negativity drains people of their positive energy. If you have a dark cloud hanging over you all of the time, your audience will start avoiding you. It takes self-discipline and a positive outlook to avoid having unnecessary negative conversation. But once you make the effort, people will be drawn to you naturally and listen attentively because you'll come across as happy and upbeat.

☺ **Focus more on expressing instead of impressing.** When someone tries too hard to impress others with what they know, it usually produces a negative counterproductive effect. No one likes a Know-It-All. It is a wiser strategy to concentrate on expressing your ideas enthusiastically on subjects that you know first-hand and are eager to share. People will be more naturally impressed with your love for a subject than with the actual content of your message.

☺ **Talk more in terms of his interests.** When it comes to selecting a topic for discussion, always keep in mind what it is that interests another person. The truth is that most people are motivated by what's in it for them. In addition, talk in a style which appeals more to their nature or the character of the situation at hand. Some people like to share ideas, feelings, and experiences while others may prefer more information, logic, and purpose in their discussions. Also, realize that there is an appropriate time for thinking and an appropriate time for feeling. Don't make the mistake of communicating like a thinker in a feeling moment or as a feeler in a moment of thinking.

☺ **Beware of too much drama.** A wise conversationalist will use the appropriate level of emotion for the message he or she is trying to convey. If too much emotion is put on insignificant things of little or no consequence — like an innocent off-color remark from a complete stranger — then a man is likely to lose his respect for the speaker and have his interest wane. Unless the man seems to be in the same mood for drama, assume that this will more than likely cause him to tune you out.

☺ **No long storytelling!** Lengthy, uninterrupted stories will usually bore your listening audience. A smart communicator trims away the fat and gives listeners the shortest possible version of their stories. This is done by cutting out the details and getting right to the action of the story. Make sure that you inject pauses that give your listeners an opportunity to comment or ask a question. If necessary, you may want to preface your story by saying, "This will only take a minute" or "Here's a quick story." This opening tells listeners how long your tale is going to be, and it alleviates the burden of having to listen politely to a potentially boring story.

☺ **Know what not to say.** We can do a lot of damage by saying too much or revealing things that are better being left unsaid. Make sure to keep any unflattering personal information off of the discussion table when you're around prospective dating candidates. In addition, qualify your more controversial remarks so that you don't come across as being too opinionated or self-righteous. That's not to say that you can't ever express your true convictions. I'm merely pointing out that in an initial social conversation, it's safer to avoid sensitive issues like politics, religion, and sex. Once you've established a solid base of rapport, there will be more appropriate times in the future when you can freely express your opinions in the fullest capacity.

☺ **Watch your audience for clues.** If your dating prospect starts to fidget, yawn, or look away from you, that may be your cue to stop talking and redirect your focus elsewhere. Just because you want to share what's on your mind, doesn't mean that the other person is in the mood to listen. Make sure that you keep him involved by asking questions and eliciting feedback throughout your conversation. Too much silence or a lack of nonverbal feedback may indicate that you've lost his attention but he's too polite to tell you to be quiet.

☺ **Adjust your volume and tone controls.** Sometimes it's not what you say that matters as much as *how* you say it. Make sure that your voice qualities are pleasing to the ears. Adjust your volume so that you're not too loud where it's annoying or too soft where it's a strain to hear you. Make sure that you enunciate clearly, and vary the pitch and speed of your speaking voice so that you don't become monotone. Even a successful actress like Heather Locklear had to take voice lessons early in her career to improve her speaking effectiveness. So become more aware of your vocal patterns, and work on improving them.

⊛ **Find the proper "air-time balance."** Some people are more comfortable listening than talking, while others are just the opposite. At the beginning of a relationship, try to find out what the other person is most comfortable with. For example, my girlfriend Nora is more comfortable in the role of a listener than a talker. With her, I often take the lead and speak more than listen. But I've also dated women who prefer talking most of the time, and in these situations, I make the proper initial adjustment by listening more and talking less.

Talking to men is speaking to an entirely different kind of audience than you do with your girlfriends. Speak to the men you meet in a manner that grabs their attention, keeps them entertained, and leaves them with a favorable impression. That way, you'll have them eager and ready for your next conversation.

Keeping men tuned in when you speak is about shifting your style so that you get them to respond. Try to do this instead of just carelessly blurting out your message without considering your audience, which usually ends up being ineffective and frustrating.

WHAT TO DO NOW

Make it a priority to focus on your conversational skills and to make improvements where necessary. Start by being brief and letting the other person do their share of the talking. Make sure that you don't dominate your conversations to the point where the other person is not equally engaged.

For pointers on how to express yourself better, take a closer look at how television talk show hosts such as Oprah Winfrey, David Letterman, Ellen DeGeneres, Conan O'Brien, Jane Pauley, Larry King, Dr. Phil McGraw, and Jay Leno communicate to their guests and audiences. Notice how they use their bodies with facial expressions, hand gestures, eye contact, body postures, and head tilts. Observe these skillful communicators as they vary their voice speed, pitch, and volume to capture our attention.

> "A gossip is one who talks to you about others;
> a bore is one who talks to you about himself;
> and a brilliant conversationalist is one who
> talks to you about yourself."
>
> Lisa Kirk
> American singer and musical comedy artist

With good role models and a commitment to constant improvement, we can all become better conversationalists in a short period of time. Get started on improving your communications with the next person you meet today.

THE BOTTOM LINE

Dating sucks when you come across as a poor conversationalist and men don't pay much attention to you. But dating rocks when a wide choice of high-quality love prospects are tuned in to you and small talk becomes an enjoyable experience for everyone involved.

Eleven

The Good Audience

DATING ROCKS WHEN YOU'RE
AN OUTSTANDING LISTENER

"Listening is a magnetic and strange
thing, a creative force. You can see that
when you think how the friends that
really listen to us are the ones we move
toward, and we want to sit in their
radius as though it did us good,
like ultraviolet rays."

Brenda Ueland
Author of *Strength to Your Sword Arm* (1993)

lis•ten•ing: 1. to tune in with the intention of hearing something. 2. the most practical way of showing sincere appreciation in a conversation. 3. where smart women excel in their effort to improve communications with men.

An honest male perspective: One trait that most men value highly in a woman is her ability to listen well and remain interested in what they have to say. Listening may be the most subtle, yet effective way of showing sincere appreciation for another person.

I had a chance to see the legendary rock band Crosby, Stills & Nash in Los Angeles during their 2004 summer concert tour. I've always been a big fan of their unique blend of tasteful lyrics, beautiful melodies, soaring harmonies, and interesting mix of personalities and musical backgrounds.

The concert I attended featured a lot of their classic hits such as "Love the One You're With," "Teach Your Children," "Just a Song Before I Go," and "Woodstock," but it also included a surprising number of fresh new songs.

After one especially catchy new tune, founding band member David Crosby said to the largely over-40 audience, "As a singer-songwriter, you can't believe how good it feels to hear you respond like that to our new music."

Whether you're attending a music concert or listening to someone talk, it is important to realize that being an attentive and appreciative audience has a tremendous effect on making the performer feel valued and important.

What Is Your Purpose In Listening?

You will find in today's fast-paced world that most people are often unaware of how good or poor they are as listeners. In most cases, the real purpose in a casual conversation is to have an enjoyable exchange that involves active participation from both parties. But many people make the common mistake of having their conversations turn into a proving ground for showing off how witty, intelligent, entertaining, or charming they are.

For those of you who fall in to this pattern, it might be useful to know that the opposite behavior may actually create the results you want. Interestingly, a natural way to impress another person is to first be impressed with that other person. By helping the other person feel the way they want to feel first, you will be in a position to have the same feeling reciprocated.

For a smart woman looking to develop her dating skills and relationship chances, it is important to do all she can to become a better listener and a more appreciative audience. In this way, she can make her everyday conversations a more pleasurable experience for anyone involved.

Who Are The Notoriously Poor Listeners?

American men (particularly those with Type-A personalities) are usually guilty of being poorer listeners than their female counterparts. One of the sports fans who comes to our weekly men's "Monday Night Football" gatherings is such a poor listener that it often becomes annoying just to have a conversation when he is there.

For example, there are nights when I begin to share a story from my life with the guys who've come over for the Monday Night Football ritual. Invariably, if our poor-listening friend is around, he will butt in with: "So what's your point, Steve?" Other times, he'll try to one-up me and say something like: "That's nothing! I've got an even better story."

While most people are not as extreme as my poor-listening friend, many find that being a good listener doesn't come easily. In fact, good listeners are hard to find these days because it's a lot easier to speak than it is to listen. Frequently, we all are guilty of paying attention to a speaker just long enough to gain a general sense of what he or she is saying. Then we turn off our ears and start formulating our own replies.

The problem with this bad habit is that we often assume we already know the speaker's point without really registering their ideas in our own heads.

Meanwhile, the speaker feels like the bad listener doesn't value what he or she is saying. And even more importantly, the person talking may wonder if the listener views them as a *person worth valuing.*

SMART MOVE #11: BECOME AN OUTSTANDING LISTENER

With the proper awareness and practice, we can all become better listeners, show more appreciation, and make deeper connections with other people. To help you make immediate progress in this area, here are some simple guidelines to follow:

Ⓟ **Give the gift of sincere listening.** Sometimes it's comforting for a speaker to share their emotional load with another person. When someone is there to listen, it fills that person's human need to be understood. Certainly, there are times when we talk about things that are not that interesting to someone else. However, their willingness to absorb our thoughts, ideas, and emotions can be both soothing and validating. Listening is seen as a true sign of caring, friendship, and even love.

Ⓟ **Set your intention on paying full attention.** Some people get easily distracted when another person is speaking. But if you become distracted, the speaker won't feel that you value what they have to say. If you want to become an outstanding listener, the first order of business is to become determined to develop the habit of giving speakers your full, undivided attention. You can accomplish this by: (1) looking them directly in the eye as they are talking, (2) keeping your body still and not fidgeting, (3) turning your body towards them instead of away, and (4) keeping quiet until they are finished completing their thoughts.

Ⓟ **Provide positive nonverbal feedback.** Show you are listening attentively by offering feedback as if that person was the only one left on this earth. You can do this by: (1) nodding your head in agreement, (2) leaning closer to the one who is speaking, (3) smiling with delight or approval, and (4) maintaining eye contact throughout the conversation. As any person with a hearing disability can verify, listening is not always an auditory communication.

"My sister has the attention span of a fly when it comes to listening to others. When you try to tell her a story about yourself, you better speak real fast. That's because she usually interrupts or changes the topic altogether. The funny thing is her best friend is the exact same way. The two of them recently had a fight because both of them are tired of the other one focusing on themselves. They made up recently, but isn't that just hilarious? By the way, they are both over forty years old, and have always been totally single."

An example of how poor listening habits can adversely affect a woman's social life

☺ **Try not to interrupt while he's speaking.** When you interrupt someone while they're talking, you are often trying to finish their sentences to speed up their story. But mostly you're in your own head thinking about what you want to talk about instead of listening. After a while, the speaker becomes annoyed by your interruptions. In order to make a speaker feel appreciated, it is important to be more patient and disciplined while listening. If necessary, ask if you can make a brief comment on their topic before letting them continue.

☺ **Help the talker get into their flow.** When I worked as a public speaking coach years ago, one of my primary tasks was to get people to talk about subjects that they were eager to discuss. I'd get things rolling by prompting with, "So John, tell us what happened to you the other day." When the speaker got stuck, I'd interject, "So what happened next?" By doing this, I was able to help the talker get into a flow. I only interrupted to get them back on track or to suggest that they elaborate on their story. If you can help other people get "in the flow" when they speak, they'll have a special appreciation for you.

☺ **Seek first to understand others instead of wanting yourself to be understood.** Most people wish others would understand them, but more rarely do we ever think about trying to understand the other person. But by turning this habit around in conversations and understanding the other person first, we can learn what is important to them early in the game. This adjustment will naturally result in conversations that are tailored to the other person's liking, and it allows for a better exchange of ideas. By shifting the focus more on the other person, we learn more about them while helping them feel more appreciated. The other person will also perceive you as being a more caring and less self-centered individual.

☞ **Repeat their words back to yourself.** A simple way to prevent yourself from filtering out what another person is saying is to repeat it in your mind while they talk. Try it! I think you'll find that this simple technique will keep your mind from wandering off. It will also help your concentration and improve your recall of what is being said.

☞ **Don't jump to conclusions!** In resolving conflicts, make sure that you hear a person out completely. Come to see their side of the story, and find out precisely what their true intentions were. That way, you can avoid the common mistake of jumping to conclusions by listening to only the early part. When you gather all the information from them, you'll be more likely to identify with the reasoning or purpose in the other person's behavior.

☞ **Ask empowering questions.** By listening more closely, you'll be able to ask the right kind of questions. Good questions either get the speaker to elaborate more fully or steer them in a more productive direction. Helpful queries include: "What made you feel really proud about that?" and "What did you enjoy the most about what happened then?" You can also empower the speaker by directing them toward subjects associated with positive emotions rather than negative ones. Instead of asking questions just for your own benefit, do so with the added intent of steering the speaker toward feeling better about themselves.

By mastering these simple listening techniques with practice and purpose, a smart woman can distinguish herself. Men you date will come to think of you as someone they can enjoy spending quality time with while doing the most basic activity — having a one-on-one casual conversation.

WHAT TO DO NOW

Take a moment and think of the best listener that you know. What are the qualities that make him or her such a great listener? Decide on at least one aspect of good listening to use in your next conversation.

Now think of someone that you regard as a poor listener. What are the qualities that make them a poor listener in your opinion? Decide on at least one aspect of poor listening that you will be careful not to use in another one of your next conversations.

At the end of each of your conversations, make sure that you notice the difference between your old style of listening and the new effects of being an outstanding listener. Now think of how much this will mean to you in terms of improving your future relationships.

THE BOTTOM LINE

Dating sucks when people start avoiding you because you've gained a reputation for being a terrible audience. But dating rocks when others feel understood and appreciated by the simple way that you listen to them.

Twelve

Meeting Men

DATING ROCKS WHEN YOU ATTRACT LOTS OF LOVE PROSPECTS

"Nothing is so often irretrievably
missed as an opportunity
we encounter every day."

Marie von Ebner-Eschenbach
Author of *Aphorisms* (1893)

op•por•tu•ni•ty: 1. a favorable or advantageous combination of circumstances. 2. a chance to advance or progress toward a desired outcome or goal. 3. what women need to make the most of when it comes to meeting quality men for love.

An honest male perspective: Opportunities are infinite for those who develop their ability to anticipate. You never know when the next person you meet might be "The One."

According to the United States Census Bureau, women make up almost 51% of the population. And it turns out that for most of the dating populace of ages 30 to 44, the number of single men and women in their region is about equal.

However, if you're a single woman living in either Alaska, Nevada, Colorado, Wyoming, Hawaii, Idaho, or Utah, you are "looking for love in all the right places." These states have the most favorable female-to-male ratios for single women in the nation.

On the other hand, a single woman living in Rhode Island, Massachusetts, or Washington, D.C., might encounter stiffer competition because these areas offer the least advantageous female-to-male ratios in the country.

While these national statistics make for interesting conversation, the reality for every woman is that you only really need to find one man in order to complete your love equation. In order to have a large pool of potential male love candidates, a smart woman needs to make the most of the social opportunities that come her way.

But what most people don't realize is that social opportunities often lie within easy range of our everyday lives. All that we have to do is become more conscious of what's going on around us, plus develop simple strategies for taking advantage of favorable circumstances.

WHEN WOMEN GET IN A DATING RUT

A woman sent the following story to me about her personal challenge of meeting quality men for dating and love:

"I've been in a dating rut for about nine months. The last two guys I dated were very hurtful to me, and so I guess I've been afraid of getting hurt again. I haven't been looking for men in any conscious sense. I will go out with my friends, but mostly to neighborhood pubs. I'll hang out with these friends all night, and then be disappointed when I don't meet any guys that I like. It feels like I've fallen out of the 'dating zone' and I can't figure out how to get back in. It's as if I've lost all of my dating confidence. I'm attractive and, by all accounts, a good catch. But my luck at meeting good men has really gone bad. Help!"

My response to this gal was that it usually takes more than luck to be successful at anything at life. Needing more than luck is especially true for a woman when it comes to finding a good man to date for a long-term committed relationship once she's exhausted her normal social resources.

BECOME PROACTIVE ABOUT MEETING MEN

In order to make the most of your social opportunities, you'll need to position yourself in the right situations. You want to go to places where a comfortable conversation could be initiated that would result in getting asked out for a real one-on-one date. Sometimes this may involve making the first move. Despite what some other dating experts might advise, I'd say that being assertive when it comes to meeting men is not only acceptable for women, but downright street-smart in many situations.

What doesn't work well is when a woman comes across as being aggressive and desperate. The normal scenario is for the man to chase and be the aggressor, while the woman entices the man to pursue her by positioning herself as approachable. For most women, being proactive means being in the right place at the most advantageous time, but from then on letting things come to her.

Additionally, as long as a woman avoids placing too much pressure on herself, there's freedom for her to pretty much do whatever she pleases, whenever she wants, and with whomever she chooses. By being proactive in this manner, she can pursue her dating interests without coming off as being overly aggressive.

OBEY THE LAW OF INDIRECT EFFECT

One reason that women fail in their "hunt" for a man is that they don't understand a concept called the "Law of Indirect Effort." Simply stated, this law says that most people achieve successful outcomes not by direct effort, but as a by-product of doing something that they enjoy.

In order to apply the Law of Indirect Effort to her dating life, a woman will have to redirect her focus away from simply meeting a man. Instead she'll want to be engaged in activities that are interesting, pleasurable, or useful to her. These activities might include such things as attending investment seminars, playing in a coed volleyball league, or going with a friend on a weekend getaway to a popular resort in order to relax and lounge by the pool.

By changing her approach in this way, a woman is able to meet men when their guard is down. Also, it can feel natural and comfortable to meet someone through one's activities and interests.

Perhaps it is the violation of the "Law of Indirect Effort" that causes some people to fail at dating. In opposition to this law are such direct approaches to connecting as matchmaking services, social clubs, and online personal ads.

SMART MOVE #12: MAXIMIZE YOUR SOCIAL OPPORTUNITIES

Here are some simple ideas to help you get out of your dating rut quickly:

☺ **Assemble a good team.** You can make this search for eligible men a lot more fun by putting together a group of like-minded friends to socialize with. Good candidates for your team would include those who: (1) keep your spirits up, (2) take you to new places, (3) share the attention, (4) say good things about you in your absence, (5) protect you from unflattering remarks, and (6) help to keep your dating standards up.

☺ **Cultivate the workplace.** According to an article that appeared in *U.S. News & World Report*, about one-third of all romances start on the job. The magazine estimated that between 6 million and 8 million Americans get involved in a romance with a fellow employee each year. And it states that about 50% of all office romances turn into lasting relationships or marriage. Some helpful activities that are related to work include: (1) meeting people in nearby offices, (2) going to company social events, (3) taking career advancement classes, and (4) going out to lunch in popular places near your workplace. Your chances also increase if lots of men are employed at your place of work and in your type of business.

☺ **Involve yourself in sports and the outdoors.** Active men typically enjoy participating in sports and being outdoors when the weather permits. You can find men at play in lots of different activities — golf, tennis, skiing, softball, volleyball, biking, jogging, bowling, fly-fishing, billiards, auto racing, touch football, and basketball, to name a few. A woman doesn't necessarily have to partake in these sports. She can just as easily be a spectator and be close to men while they're playing their favorite sport.

☺ **Eat, drink, and be merry.** One of the most convenient ways to meet men is while they're having a good time drinking, eating, or celebrating. Some options to consider include happy hours, sushi bars, oyster bars, sports bars, karaoke bars, coffee houses, your town's best delicatessen, the place that serves the best buffalo wings, an Irish pub, or any place with a popular bartender and a lively crowd.

☺ **Circulate around the travel scene.** It's easy to run into people while on vacation at such locations as tropical destinations, cruise ships, ski resorts, and luxury hotels. You can also strike up a conversation while traveling on a train, bus, airplane, ferry, subway, or airport shuttle. In addition, consider visiting tourist attractions in your area such as wineries, aquariums, museums, galleries, cultural events, and historical sites. Keep in mind that while men may be easier to meet and interact with on the travel scene, that doesn't mean that these men are good love candidates for you to consider seriously.

℗ **Get a little help from your friends.** Friends and family may be your best resource for finding and meeting new dating prospects. They can often make an easy connection for you with someone who is prequalified as a good possibility. It helps to have more than one group of friends to associate with so you can meet a variety of people. Otherwise, you will quickly exhaust your supply of possible men for dating.

℗ **Explore your neighborhood.** Make sure that you don't overlook the importance of proximity when it comes to meeting people. If you live in an area that has an abundance of single men, be on the lookout for chance encounters at coffee houses, grocery stores, dry cleaning establishments, banks, breakfast hangouts, postal/shipping centers, laundromats, health foods stores, hair salons that cater to both men and women, gourmet delicatessens, school events, car washes, dog-walking trails, and movie rental stores. If you don't live an area that has a good number of single men, then you should consider spending more time in sections of your town that do.

℗ **Look for potential shopping encounters.** I believe it's true that most men don't enjoy the adventure of shopping as much as women do. However, it would be a mistake for women to think that men don't like to spend money on things that interest them. A smart women will often find men with their guard down in places that sell sporting goods, computers, home-improvement items, automobiles, electronic gadgets, books, magazines, music, men's clothes, and business-travel items.

☞ **Expand your leisure activities.** Successful men are known to work hard, play hard, think hard, and contribute to worthy causes. When a man has free time, don't expect him to sit around his apartment and watch television (except football!) or curl up to a good book. Instead, be on the lookout for men doing a wide variety of leisure activities. You might find men with their guard down at antique car shows, performance driving schools, outdoor music festivals, racetracks and casinos, computer classes, investment seminars, charity pancake breakfasts, college events, political fund-raisers, radio-station promotional events, swap meets, and various church activities.

☞ **Go online for dating prospects.** If you have a positive attitude about online dating, then there's no denying that this medium offers a good chance for success. Online dating is particularly suited for people who tend to be shy or who live in small communities and want to branch out. If you're going to try online dating, be sure to do it in a smart way by designing an effective personal profile, being patient with your prospects, maintaining a safe approach, and finding the right online service that suits your style.

Do a variety of worthwhile activities in order to have an abundant flow of diverse new dating prospects. The more you get out there, the more possibilities you will have. Do this while remembering that you only have to find one good man in order to make your love life complete.

What To Do Now

Your first task associated with this chapter is to make a new friend. This friend is someone who will eventually introduce you to the people, places, and activities of their life. Your second task is to take part in a new activity that involves interacting with people. This could be centered around work, school, sports, hobbies, or leisure. The third task is for you to move one of your favorite activities into a new time slot. This will allow you to keep doing what you love, but with a chance of meeting a different group of like-minded people.

The final task is for you to start doing something that you always wanted to do just for the fun of it. Remember, it's important to have this kind of diversion from the dating scene in order to refresh your spirit and restore your emotional balance.

Even if you don't meet your love match doing any of the suggested activities, these steps will increase your awareness and stretch your ability to meet new people. This may also make you a more interesting person who will be more attractive to the dating prospects who you do eventually meet.

The Bottom Line

Dating sucks when you're stuck in a rut and can't find any new love prospects. But dating rocks when you do a variety of interesting activities that allow you to meet lots of men with their guard down in low-pressure social situations.

Thirteen

Competition

DATING SUCKS WHEN YOU BATTLE TOO HARD FOR ATTENTION

"The great disadvantage of being
in a rat race is that it is humiliating.
The competitors in a rat race are,
by definition, rodents."

Margaret Halsey
Author of *The Folks at Home* (1952)

com•pe•ti•tion: 1. the act of contending against another or others for a profit or prize. 2. a rivalry between two or more entities striving for the same objective. 3. what smart women need to deal with effectively when they want the attention of a man that other women also want.

An honest male perspective: Competition exists whether you like it or not! It has a lot to do with our natural tendency as human beings to make comparisons. It makes perfect sense for you to do all that you can in order to compare favorably to other women in physical, emotional, mental, social, and spiritual ways. Still, competing wisely does not mean that you have to become a "dog eat dog" competitor. It's more about making sure that you get a fair chance to shine.

The hit romantic reality-show *The Bachelor* features a handsome, likeable, and successful single man searching for the woman of his dreams. He meets 25 women with the stated intention that one of them will eventually become his bride.

The Bachelor follows a gradual process of elimination during which the man narrows down the field of contending bachelorettes from 25 to 15 in the first episode. He indicates his choices ceremoniously by presenting those he wants to get to know better with a single red rose. Each week, the bachelor continues to explore and eliminate more women until the last episode; finally, he must make his crucial choice from the last two remaining women. At this point, the stakes are high — real emotions are involved!

The Bachelor is made for television. There is heightened drama, fantasy dates, unrealistic dating odds, and a poor track-record for marriage success. None of the previous five bachelors have married or remained with the woman that they selected. However, the show provides a fascinating view of our culture's dating rituals. Evidently, lots of women like the "fairy tale" aspects of the show even though the odds of success for the resulting couple are so low.

In the sixth edition of *The Bachelor*, Byron Velvick, a 40-year-old professional bass fisherman from Nevada, proposed to Mary Delgado, a 36-year-old real estate agent from Florida. This joyful occasion occurred after a long and competitive ordeal, which at times brought out unsavory catty qualities in some of the female contestants.

As a man observing this show, I find it sad to see a gal who slams other women viciously in her pursuit of winning a romantic competition. While this type of ugly behavior is occasionally seen among men, it seems to be a more common occurrence between women in today's dating world.

Perhaps this behavior starts early in a young girl's life because of poor self-confidence or feelings of unworthiness. Stories of teenage girls being vicious towards other girls are commonplace and aren't restricted to romantic situations — in fact, the 2004 movie *Mean Girls* was even based on this theme. Unfortunately, some women never seem to learn that they can get what they want in life without stepping all over someone else.

If an enlightened woman wants to find a love that works, she must choose a code of conduct that allows her to gain the attention of potential suitors without ruining her spirit with the ill side-effects of nasty competition. My advice is to be the kind of person you want to attract. Remember that negative emotions naturally attract negative qualities. You attract who you are, not necessarily who you want.

IS COMPETITION STILL A BIG ISSUE FOR YOU?

When I was in high school, competition for the attention of the opposite sex was a common thing for both young men and women. What girl could possibly compete against the Homecoming Queen? Or what boy could expect to outshine the Captain of the football team? Even as mature adults, we can still face challenges similar to the ones that were so difficult to deal with back in high school.

Here's an example of how one woman has dealt effectively with competition in her adult dating-life:

> "Personally, I think there is a big difference between 'being competitive' and competing directly against another woman. I am competitive in the sense that my health, style, grooming, and general attractiveness are all important to me. I want to be at my very best. Men are attracted to women who take care of themselves and radiate self-confidence. On the other hand, men don't like women who undermine other women directly. My philosophy is that a woman should present herself as the man's best choice. If he's still interested in other women, then either accept that you're not the one for him at that moment in time, keep the relationship at the 'We're just having fun' stage, or just move on quietly. It's the drama that's associated with competing directly against other women that's so demeaning."

Even though competition exists around you in some form from time to time, it doesn't mean that you have to respond with ugliness or pettiness. Instead, choose to respond in ways that help you to keep cool while looking your best for potential suitors.

GET YOURSELF WELL POSITIONED

The simplest way to make an impression on a prospective love partner is to be "first on the scene." When two people meet, are receptive to each other, and neither one is in love with someone else, then the chances that love could occur are good. If you're the first woman to appeal to a man's heart, then it's just a matter of making sure that you don't create reasons for him to switch his loyalties.

Being first also applies to other phases in dating as well; these include exchanging contact information, getting a date, and becoming intimate. The first woman who makes a strong emotional impact on a man when he's feeling both a tug on his heart and intense desire remains there until proven otherwise.

SMART MOVE #13: HANDLE COMPETITION EFFECTIVELY

In addition to being first, here are other ways to respond effectively in a competitive dating situation:

⌘ **Be truly outstanding at something.** Making a great first impression is more than having nothing wrong with you. If you want to create positive impact, make sure that there is something fabulous about you that stands out from the crowd. For instance, you may have tremendous self-confi-

Your Ideal Social Team

ARE YOU ASSOCIATING WITH THE RIGHT CROWD?
It's time to size up those who you choose to socialize with.

CONTAGIOUS POSITIVE ATTITUDE
- Physical Energy   Poor   Fair   Good   Excellent
- Enthusiasm & Optimism   Poor   Fair   Good   Excellent
- Fun & Sense of Humor   Poor   Fair   Good   Excellent
- Feelings towards Men   Poor   Fair   Good   Excellent
- Willingness to Try New Things   Poor   Fair   Good   Excellent
- Compassion towards Women   Poor   Fair   Good   Excellent
- Keep Your Standards High   Poor   Fair   Good   Excellent

WINNING TEAM CONCEPT
- Share the Attention   Poor   Fair   Good   Excellent
- Share the Good Prospects   Poor   Fair   Good   Excellent
- Share the Conversation   Poor   Fair   Good   Excellent
- Appreciate Your Gifts   Poor   Fair   Good   Excellent
- Sell You When You're Absent   Poor   Fair   Good   Excellent
- Willingness to Defend You   Poor   Fair   Good   Excellent
- Availability to Your Needs   Poor   Fair   Good   Excellent

BONUS FACTORS
- Maturity & Responsibility   Poor   Fair   Good   Excellent
- Connected to Other Networks   Poor   Fair   Good   Excellent
- Shared Moral Values   Poor   Fair   Good   Excellent
- Mutual Safety Concerns   Poor   Fair   Good   Excellent
- Common Sense & Awareness   Poor   Fair   Good   Excellent
- Matching Dating Goals   Poor   Fair   Good   Excellent

Points:		Total Score:		
Excellent	4	60-80	A Great Crowd!
Good	3	45-59	Good Part-Timers
Fair	2	30-44	Not Much Help
Poor	0	0-29	Leave Behind Now!

THE BOTTOM LINE
Enjoy the dating process more by associating with good people.

dence, personal style, a sense of humor, the ability to listen, or physical vitality.

🕉 **Master your auditory channel.** There are usually limits to how much better you can look compared to other women. However, there is almost no conscious competition when it comes to how well you can communicate with appealing voice qualities and well-chosen words. If you want a level playing-field when competing against otherwise tough rivals, consider becoming outstanding at communicating with pleasant sounding voice-qualities. This is a hidden way of making a powerful unconscious impression on your dating prospects.

🕉 **Associate with the right crowd.** The friends that you choose can have a great effect on your success with dating. You are often judged by the company you keep. Plus, your friends can promote you or tear you down in your absence. In addition, some friends provide support and encouragement, while others drain your energy and make you feel less sure about your chances for love. Most of all, my advice is to never underestimate the power of influence. It is often subtle, but also it can be quite powerful. A woman is rarely much more optimistic about romance than the peer group that she spends the most time around. (Refer to the opposite page for ideas on the qualities to seek out.)

🕉 **Don't say it or show it in public.** If you can't say anything positive about another person, then it's a wise policy to not say anything at all. This is particularly true when it comes to discussing other women in the presence of men. Whatever you say or do is often replayed out of context to a less receptive audience. Distortions in meaning, intent, or significance will most likely make you look awful in the final analysis.

☞ **Search for the humor.** If you can find what's funny in an otherwise challenging moment, you can break the competitive tension and free your energies for more important purposes. Most dating competition occurs early and an unwise competitor can put too much significance on the initial feedback. In the beginning, it's usually best to keep the emotions light and the pressure to compete minor.

☞ **Don't ever let the means justify the ends.** In life, a person rarely gets to keep what they don't deserve. This is particularly true when it comes to competing for love. If you get the love of a man by dishonest or unkind actions, then those same qualities will eventually reappear and cause negative effects in the relationship. Rather than trying to decide what is most advantageous for you, the wiser policy is to simply refrain from actions that you can't be proud of and know are not right. You're better off realizing that "what goes around comes around" and initiating positive actions and healthy behaviors that ensure favorable long-term results.

☞ **Outclass your rivals.** Maintaining your dignity and poise in times of stress will separate you from your competition. While others resort to desperate acts to tear you down, rise above this kind of demeaning warfare and choose not to engage in these unhealthy battles. A woman's ability to remain strong, yet flexible, in times of adversity is highly valued by enlightened men looking for an emotionally mature love-partner. Any time you choose to play by someone else's rules, you lose — force them to play by yours.

By following these general guidelines, you can handle your competitive challenges with more control and less worry. In addition, your more perceptive or refined male suitors often will notice the resourceful and stylish manner in which you handle a competitive environment.

What To Do Now

Think of a time when you didn't handle competition in the way that you would have liked. What gave you that feeling? Was it the effect that you had on other people, the outcome you received, or maybe the sense within yourself of not being at your best? What specific lessons did you learn from this previous experience with competition?

Now look back at that time with the added understanding that you currently possess. How would you handle the situation differently? When you are faced with a similar challenge, what will you be absolutely certain to do and not do the next time around?

Finally, let your next opportunity to compete be a chance to let your dignity and emotional maturity shine brilliantly through the clouds of adversity brought on by fierce, unenlightened competitors.

The Bottom Line

Dating sucks when you are trying too hard to win the attention of prospective love partners. But dating rocks when you can handle unfriendly, misguided, unfair, or even unbeatable competition with dignity and class.

Fourteen

Early Stages

DATING ROCKS WHEN YOU CONTROL THE PACE AND DIRECTION

"I feel that the moment a date happens that it is a social encounter. And the question of sex needs to be negotiated from the first moment on."

Camille Paglia
Author of *Sex, Art, and American Culture* (1992)

ear•ly stag•es: 1. the first steps or phases in a process, series or development. 2. in the context of romantic love relationships, the first days, weeks, and months of dating. 3. when a woman is going out with, dating, or seeing a man, but before he becomes her exclusive boyfriend.

An honest male perspective: People ruin their chances for real love by wanting too much too soon. You are wise to let love unfold naturally rather than trying to force it into your own time-table. By the same token, if you're not getting measurable results in a reasonable amount of time, you should begin looking for alternatives to the love situation you're in.

In March 1998, I attended a two-day seminar, "How to Create a Mega Best-Selling Book," presented by Mark Victor Hansen and Jack Canfield, the creators of the *Chicken Soup for the Soul* series of books.

At the time, I had a general idea for a dating book and wanted to learn more about how to turn that idea into a reality. Like many of the novices at the seminar, I thought that all an aspiring author had to do was write a manuscript, get a publisher to print it, and then sit back and relax while collecting the royalties. But the seminar gave me several new distinctions about the various things that go into creating a successful book project.

The early stages of creating a book were of particular interest to me because I had been stuck in the novice phase for several years. I learned that writing a successful book requires an author to set personal goals, select a marketable topic, create a clever book title, research the topic thoroughly, test and retest ideas, and improve the body of work until it meets the standards of the professional book trade.

Without a complete understanding of the early stages of book development, a new author has little chance of writing a book that will sell in today's market. In addition, a book that doesn't have strong chances of selling will not attract any interest from cost-conscious, profit-minded publishers. Therefore, it is important for every aspiring author to focus on the early stages of development.

In a similar way, a smart woman needs a thorough understanding of the early stages in developing a fulfilling love relationship. To the novice, it may seem like this task is a simple matter of a boy meeting a girl. But for a woman who wants to improve her chances for long-term success at love, it's important to pass through each step in the early stages properly. That's because too many mistakes repeated often will keep a love-thirsty woman stuck and frustrated in the early dating stages forever.

Appreciate Your Time In The Early Stages

Many people don't seem to understand the simple principle in life that things of value require time to develop. Like fine wine, love relationships often take time to grow and ripen properly.

Here is an example of how one woman describes the way that she rushes herself in her dating life:

> "I've got a big problem in that I always rush in and fall in love too fast. I just have an uncanny way of

159

confessing my love too soon, and scaring off the guy I like. I just rented a movie titled *How to Lose a Guy in 10 Days*, and I should have played the leading role because I'm a total expert at losing them. Now that I'm not involved with anyone, I can clearly see the mistakes I've made and why I don't ever want to repeat them. Most people say that the woman should control the pace of the relationship. But it seems like guys can do this more easily because they seem so much better at not rushing in and revealing their feelings too soon."

My response to this woman is that the pace and direction of a love relationship should be in sync with both the man *and* the woman. The urge to rush ahead, whether it be physically or emotionally, must be tempered in order for a love to develop and mature naturally.

The best strategy is to remain on the right course in order to create a love that will be good for both parties. Staying on a wise course includes keeping a pace that allows each person to get to know the other, become comfortable, and develop certainty about whether the relationship will work.

By watching for obvious clues in the early stages of dating, a smart woman can avoid deeper involvement in unfavorable love situations and steer herself towards the ones that have the best chances of succeeding.

"Are You Going To Date Me Or What?"

When a man meets a woman, the first thing that goes through his mind is whether he notices anything special about her or not. If he has no strong, favorable impression of her, then there isn't much hope that this particular guy will date the woman any time soon.

But if he forms a positive initial impression, the man will then further evaluate how strongly he feels about her. That means the man will determine if he is attracted enough to her to make a concerted effort to overcome his fear of rejection, if necessary.

If everything falls into place, then the next logical step for the man is to address the issue of contact information. He may ask for (or give her) a phone number or email address, or he may suggest that they exchange such details.

What confuses a lot of women is when a man asks for this information and then doesn't make contact again. The woman assumes that such men ask because they want to date them, when that isn't always the case. A man may only want the opportunity to date a woman and postpone the evaluation of that opportunity until a later time. He may have his own personal drawbacks when it comes to dating a woman; his stumbling blocks might include such things as already being involved with or wanting to be involved with another woman, not having the time and/or money to date in the style he prefers, and not feeling emotionally ready to finish something that he starts.

Some guys will even send an email, leave a text message, or make a phone call to a woman in this pre-dating stage just to get a feeling for whether he's comfortable with the idea of dating her. He may also want to check if she's likely to say "yes" to such a request for one-on-one time. The man might not have the intention of asking her out right away.

At this point, the man has to measure whether his interest in the woman outweighs the collective fears, doubts, and hassles (money, time, effort, comfort level) related to actually ask her out. If a guy wastes too much time in this pre-dating stage, then any self-respecting woman should stop wasting her energies and shift her focus towards other prospects.

An alternative for a gutsy woman who doesn't want to mess around waiting for an ambivalent guy to make up his mind is to cut to the chase by asking him directly: "*So are you going to date me or what?*"

SMART MOVE #14: CONTROL THE PACE AND DIRECTION

As you've observed from the previous discussion, a man goes through a series of evaluations to determine if he will proceed in his pursuit of a woman. When his feelings aren't strong enough, expect him to cut back his pursuit, do a slow fade out, or simply disappear.

Here are some important things for any woman to consider if she wants to control the pace and direction of the dating relationship in the early stages:

🕭 **Help him make the first move.** As a general rule, set it up so that the man makes the first move. You can provide suggestions and encouragement in order to make this easier for him, but he is the one who has to pass the twin tests of desire and courage. If he doesn't have much of either, then this isn't a guy who deserves your efforts.

🕭 **Get him comfortable first.** Men don't like to look stupid and will do almost anything to avoid being too far outside of their comfort zone. This means that a woman should lower the pressure of dating to a point where it is casual enough to put him at ease. However, don't make the event seem so trivial that he will take it too lightly.

☺ **Is he a decent guy?** All good dating prospects are quality human beings. So the first thing that you have to determine is whether the fellow you're interested in is a decent person or not. Associating in any expanded way with an unhealthy individual is a sure-fire formula for disaster.

☺ **Is he a good love-candidate?** While all good love candidates are good guys, not all good guys make good love candidates for you. You have to be a good match for him and he has to be a good match for you as well. Aside from feeling that you are the right woman and he is the right man, you should also make sure that there aren't any major divisive issues (race, religion, ethnicity, family, economics, distance, schedules, etc.) that could make the long-term situation too difficult to overcome.

☺ **Remember, he's watching out for glaring weaknesses.** Initially, it's natural for people of both genders to wonder, "If this person is so great, then why are they still single?" Expect men to be sensitive in the beginning for what might be wrong with a new woman they are dating. A smart woman is fully aware of both minimizing the perception of what may be construed as a weakness and shifting the focus immediately towards her strengths. Redirecting his focus will help you get the relationship off the ground.

☺ **Is he getting more into you?** While it's natural to gauge whether you're getting more into the man you're dating, it is equally important to note if he's getting more interested in you. Men will typically evaluate their love for a woman heavily by their intensity of desire. If you're not feeling the heat of the chase, then you're probably not

When He's Not That Into You!

Here's a list of some common signs that the man you've met is not really interested in dating you or seeing you romantically in the future. Rather than wanting to tell you right to your face that you're not the one for him, he'll more than likely drag things along and hope that the relationship will fade away. Also, be sensitive to the opposite, which is a man who communicates in his own subtle ways with a growing interest and the desire to be the man in your life.

* He starts calling you "Dude."
* He is easily distracted or fidgets when you're talking to him.
* He doesn't ask you out on a real date.
* He doesn't pay attention to you or it's hard for him to pay attention.
* He pulls away from you in casual physical contact.
* He spends less and less time with you.
* He doesn't spend money on a real date, just hangs out with you.
* He says that he likes you but...(some lame excuse).
* He isn't motivated to have sexual contact with you.
* He doesn't show any affection towards you in public.
* He only communicates by text messages, not by voice or in person.
* He only replies to your emails and doesn't initiate them.
* He can't remember your name or anything about you.
* He makes excuses for not wanting sex with you.
* He doesn't ask any questions about you and your life.
* He doesn't open up to reveal any of his feelings, especially towards you.
* He doesn't include you in any of his plans, dreams, or fantasies.
* He doesn't do nice things for you.
* He rarely talks about "us" or "we," but mostly about "me" and "I."
* He doesn't seem to want to kiss you.
* He says that he doesn't want a relationship.
* He's always disappearing for days or weeks.
* He's always drunk or high when he wants sex with you.
* He doesn't seem to want to touch you.
* He says that he's too tired or busy with work to see you much.
* He doesn't make any sacrifices to see or talk to you.
* He doesn't introduce you to his close friends and family.
* He doesn't appear to want to be seen in public with you.
* He wants to keep long-distance romances long distance for a long time.

connecting as well as you might hope or think. If he's not that interested you, then you have zero chance to make this work and must move on regardless of how much you like him. Many people fail to understand that chemistry is something that doesn't change much over time.

꩜ **Can this work without him changing?** Sometimes a man will stop his pursuit of an attractive woman because he feels that he would have to make major changes in order to make her happy. Unsuspecting women often overlook this possibility because the man will probably be giving mostly favorable feedback on the exterior. However, on the inside, he's thinking that there is something — entirely different lifestyles, values, goals, or personalities — that will not match up well over time. Unless the man's desire is extremely high or his chances are few, he may simply pass on a woman who presents too many differences. Not going forward isn't about disliking her, it's because he doesn't want to go through the effort, frustration, and hassle of trying to change each other in order to make the relationship work long-term.

꩜ **Is hanging out a good option?** Your peer group will often determine what's cool and what's not in the case of dating. For some younger people, hanging out with friends is a low-pressure semi-date experience that determines how well you mix together in public. Generally speaking, from a woman's perspective, this is not a real date and should be done sparingly and for only a short period of time. This is not a good substitute for demonstrating a man's sincere interest in you and is primarily designed as a way to get more comfortable first or a cheap way of seeing if there's any chemistry going on.

☺ **Real dating means real risk.** When a guy has good intentions with a woman, he will willingly spend time and money to create an enjoyable dating experience. So if you don't see this in the first two one-on-one encounters, then you're probably dealing with a guy who isn't interested in having a serious relationship with you of any kind. Consider his actions at this stage carefully before proceeding any further, otherwise you may end up in a "friends with benefits" arrangement. In that type of relationship, the participants don't invest much of themselves emotionally and hence don't receive the joy that a healthy love relationship naturally provides. By going on real dates, you will quickly sort out the men who don't have serious intentions with you and therefore could care less about making a big impression on you.

☺ **Remember that sex changes everything.** The basic rule on this point is that having sex too soon hurts your chances for real love. On a more practical level, smart women should at least avoid having sex with a guy that they are interested in on the first few dates. Otherwise, you'll have to overcome the awkwardness of having too much physical intimacy without the corresponding emotions. Having sex is much more enjoyable for both parties when a gradual emotional buildup makes the physical moment feel special and right. A more mature man with sincere interest and respect for a woman will gladly wait for this special moment to happen naturally.

By increasing your knowledge of each step in the dating process, you will be able to anticipate how to respond wisely to both good and bad opportunities that come your way.

WHAT TO DO NOW

Think of a time in your dating life when you rushed things too much. Perhaps you became emotionally attached too quickly or allowed sex to happen early on. What would you do specifically in order to avoid this from happening again in the future?

Now think of a time when you may have gone too slow and lost momentum with a dating prospect. Maybe in this situation you neglected to express your true interest or didn't plan your time in order to allow feelings to take root. What would you do differently in this situation in order to give love a better chance of succeeding?

> "One should always act from one's inner sense of rhythm."
> Rosamond Lehmann
> Author of *The Ballad and the Source* (1945)

In either case, what have you learned about yourself and your natural tendencies in the early stages of dating that would be useful to know before entering into your next romantic encounter?

Remember that smart dating boils down to doing the right things, at the proper time and in a wise and patient manner.

THE BOTTOM LINE

Dating sucks when you don't have any control of either the pace or direction of your love life. But dating rocks when you have a firm grip of what's going on in each stage of your relationship. That way, you can invest your energy and emotions on men who are good prospects for lasting love.

Fifteen

Love Connections

DATING SUCKS WHEN YOU MISJUDGE HOW WELL YOU CLICK

"Most men seize up and develop
a terrible shortness of breath,
often for years, frequently for a lifetime,
before they are ever able comfortably
to say, 'I love you.' On the other hand,
beware of a man who tells you that
he loves you, especially too fast,
especially in the heat of the moment."

Betty Jane Wylie
Canadian poet and playwright

con•nec•tion: 1. the emotional state of being linked, united, or joined. 2. when two people share high levels of true chemistry rather than just temporary infatuation or attraction. 3. in the context of dating, the measure of how well you're doing as a couple in terms of bonding.

An honest male perspective: You need multiple types of attachments to a boyfriend in order to secure love for the long term. If you have an unshakable physical, emotional, mental, and spiritual love connection, you'll be able to handle the inevitable tests of adversity and adjustments to change that will come your way over time.

"Jason is an idiot. There will be no second date!" proclaimed an attractive young woman on an episode of the popular syndicated dating show, *Blind Date.*

For those who aren't familiar with this TV program, it's about the adventure of dating someone for the first time. In the segments, a newly acquainted couple travels around town doing fun things while the viewer gets to watch this often comical event unfold. An entertaining feature used in *Blind Date* is the pop-up wisecrack: these comments, which appear written on the screen in the "dialog bubble" style of comic strips, candidly suggest what the two people might be thinking about each other.

In most cases, the dates that capture our interest are the ones that don't go very well. It's especially insightful when one person is happy with the date, but their counterpart reveals that he or she doesn't feel anywhere near the same.

As you're first getting to know someone, it's important to accurately gauge how well you click with each other. That way, you'll know whether it's right to proceed any further in your romantic relationship.

Is He Really Into You — Or Not?

Men typically measure their interest in a woman heavily by their degree of sexual desire. When a guy's fervor isn't very high or sustainable, then he won't pursue a woman aggressively. What is most confusing for a woman is when a man appears to be really into her at first, keeps her strung along by saying the right things, and then just fades away.

While this seems dishonest and unkind, it's far easier for many men to completely withdraw from a situation than to tell a woman to her face that he doesn't like her or has lost his sense of attraction.

One woman sent the following story to me which illustrates this common and confusing scenario:

"I met this great guy at a conference about a year ago and clicked with him immediately. However, things didn't progress any further because we live in different cities. We stayed in contact calling each other every couple of months. Then he visited my city (Los Angeles) for business, and we were able to get together a couple times. He and I talked for hours on both occasions and had a great time. This man made it quite clear that he found me attractive. I figured that he really liked me and wanted to make a go of things. I visited him in his town (Chicago) a short while after those two get-togethers, and we had sex for the first time. It was amazing! He even wanted to cuddle and talk for hours afterwards. I visited him a few more times after that and things seemed to be going okay. Then I told him that I'd like to get a job transfer to Chicago and find an apartment so we could really be together. Now he suddenly seems like he's not that interested in me anymore. He's stopped calling me and hasn't returned my calls for a long, long time. What's going on with this guy? Are we really over and out?"

As in the example above, a lot of women are hopeful that a man who has cooled to them will change and that the romance will get better again. While being patient and having faith are strong personal qualities, sometimes you have to cut your losses. If a man is showing you clear signs that he is not into you anymore, then stop wasting your time and start over with a new guy.

LOVE BEGINS UNCONSCIOUSLY

The first connection that you make in a love relationship occurs unconsciously. You communicate it to each other through your voices, words, and body language. The rule here is that the more you demonstrate that you are similar to another person in the way you communicate, the more they tend to like you.

There is a natural rhythm that occurs on many levels when two people are in sync, especially when it comes to love. Common signs are a strong tendency to talk at the same pace and volume, to touch each other in equal amounts, to maintain the same amount of eye contact, to move at the same speed, and to have similar matches in largely unnoticed features like muscular tension, facial expressions, body posture, and breathing patterns.

If you find a man who is a mismatch for you in a lot of these usually unconscious areas, then you won't be clicking with each other for very long. This is true despite whatever honorable intentions you both may have.

SMART MOVE #15: GAUGE YOUR CONNECTION ACCURATELY

Here are some key points to help you get a more accurate read on the current condition of your love relationship:

📖 **How extensive is your sensory appeal?** A strong connection here is when both parties respond favorably to each other by the way they look, sound, feel, taste, and smell. Examples of this may include when a man: (1) especially enjoys a woman's natural scent, (2) likes the colors she wears, (3) likes to touch her skin and hair, (4) looks at her a lot from a distance, (5) replays the woman's recorded messages just to hear the sound of her voice, and (6) is delighted by a simple kiss on the cheek — just to name a few. If a strong sensory connection isn't felt by both of you, then romance will only come from forced, conscious efforts. That type of relationship will invariably fade in time or prove to be emotionally unfulfilling.

📖 **Measure both the physical *and* emotional intensity.** In addition to his physical attraction to a woman, a man will also measure his interest for her by the emotional intensity she stirs. How strongly he feels may rise and fall at various times. For some men, the emotional highs are far more important than the lows. Like an addictive drug, some men can be drawn to a woman who rocks his world despite any negative side-effects of that relationship.

Chemistry vs. Infatuation

Infatuation is often mistaken for romantic chemistry. That's because the two appear the same in the early stages. But infatuation is a foolish attachment that is fueled by passion, dreams, and the novelty of a romance. On the other hand, romantic chemistry is a deep feeling of connection that stays strong for a long time. When you're trying to gauge the strength of your love connection, be sure to put romantic chemistry at the top of your list. If it's high in the beginning, it usually stays that way unless someone destroys it through emotional immaturity. But if it's low in the start of a relationship, it rarely gets much better. Here's a list of clues which would indicate that his feelings of love for you have real staying power.

* He's always got you on his mind wherever he is and whatever he's doing.

* He's always thinking of ways to surprise and delight you.

* He gets a thrill by just looking at you or pictures of you.

* He's no longer interested in other women as romantic partners.

* He likes the idea of growing old with you.

* He enjoys touching you and being touched by you.

* He'll call you during the day just to hear your voice.

* He's grateful to the heavens that you're in his life.

* His happiest moments are ones that he gets to share with you.

* He enjoys the idea of planning things together with you.

* He doesn't have any trouble forgiving you for your mistakes.

* He feels jealous if you become strongly interested in another man.

* He felt that there was something very special about first meeting you.

* It's almost impossible for him to say "no" to you.

* He's a great listener without having to force himself with techniques.

* He enjoys himself with you regardless of the activity or circumstance.

* He makes it clear that he wants a permanent love relationship with you.

* He wants to spend as much time with you as he can.

* He experiences a unique kind of peacefulness around you.

* He wants to continue his relationship with you despite difficulties.

* His sexual interest is almost always there.

* His love persists even with frequent contact.

* Your approval means a great deal to him.

* He will strongly protect you against unfair criticism.

* He's easily satisfied with any acts of kindness from you.

* His feelings of love for you never die.

⊛ **Are you the mental equivalent?** Aside from the physical and emotional aspects of attraction, there also should be a strong mental connection. When people are of the same mind and can think alike on a variety of key issues, then there is enough mental rapport to expand on as time goes on. Without strong mental compatibility, your relationship is doomed to being a part-time activity. Eventually, each person will naturally go off to do their own thing and spend time with people who are more like-minded.

⊛ **Is the silence golden?** A characteristic of a solid spiritual connection is the ability to "just be together" sharing quiet times. It's during these experiences that you appreciate the beauty of the moment with an overwhelming sense of gratitude for the presence of someone you cherish. Choosing to sit together silently by a fireplace to enjoy the beauty and coziness of observing burning wood together is a good indication of strong love. On the other hand, an excessive need to watch television and tune each other out is not a good sign.

⊛ **Observe the conversational flow.** How do you recognize an ideal flow in communication? It's when the conversations have a natural rhythm, and each participant is joyfully involved in both roles as talker and listener. Too many short conversations, dead silence from the other side, or overuse of email and text messages may disguise a more serious flaw in the love connection.

⊛ **Appreciate the natural laughter.** When two people are in sync, there's a natural tendency to find more humor and laughter in everyday things. This isn't about being a comedian or falling for a guy with a salesman's skill of making you laugh. It's more about the closeness you feel with a certain man. The feelings that you share for each other cause you both to express yourselves joyfully in humor, laughter, and fun. An absence of joy is a sure indicator of a poor connection in the relationship.

☺ **How well do you bring out the best in each other?** When two people seem to be made for each other, there is a natural tendency for them to bring out the strengths in their partners. Whenever a woman chooses to associate closely with a love interest, she should ask herself the following questions: (1) What has he got me thinking and believing? (2) What has he got me doing? and (3) What has he got me becoming? If you absolutely know that your influence on each other is not all right, then you're not in a healthy relationship.

☺ **Does time distortion occur often?** When two people are fully connected, there are moments when time seems to zoom by quickly. These can be wonderful experiences where nothing seems to matter except the enjoyment of each other's company. As the old adage so wisely points out, time really does fly when you're having fun. Or another way of looking at this indicator is that "Time flies when you're in love."

☺ **Has he spoken the magic words?** When a man becomes completely convinced of his love for a woman, it is only natural for him to say, "I love you." Being fully connected to her opens up his heart and allows him to express his feeling for the woman fully. An absence of these magical words indicates that the man is either consumed by the fear of the consequences of saying it or by the doubt he has because of his lack of deep feelings or lower than acceptable levels of romantic chemistry.

As you get better at gauging the quality of your love connections, you'll save yourself time, effort, and emotion by avoiding dead-end romances. In addition, you'll focus on the ones that are more likely to work.

WHAT TO DO NOW

Take a good look at a past or present relationship of yours. How would you evaluate this relationship on each key point described in the preceding section? Are there clear ways that you connect or connected well? Is (was) the connection only average at best in other ways?

At some point, people skills and romantic intentions can reach a limit in terms of how much they help a love take root and grow. If measurable results are not achieved in a reasonable time, two mature adults may have to reassess their relationship and determine a new direction. Both the woman and the man can only find true happiness, passion, and fulfillment when they are connected well in several key areas. Being in a relationship for security, comfort, or to avoid being alone will never bring you the life of your dreams.

THE BOTTOM LINE

Dating sucks when don't have the foggiest idea where you stand in your relationship. But dating rocks when things are clicking on all cylinders and your love for each other gets better with each passing day, week, month, and year.

Sixteen

Part-Time Boyfriends

DATING SUCKS WHEN YOU LIMIT YOUR PARTNER'S INTEREST

"In every animal under the sun
below man as far as I know
it is the male who has to please
the female. Yet among men,
it is the opposite."

Martha Lavell
American editor and social researcher

part-time: 1. employed to work or be used for less than the usual amount. 2. lasting, requiring, or being in force for a specific function and only for a limited time. 3. in the context of a love relationship, a partner who only devotes a portion of their time, focus, and energy to you.

An honest male perspective: Expand rather than limit your partner's interest in you and the relationship by developing common interests that you can both enjoy together. Remaining stuck in too many activities that a man doesn't like will surely reduce your time with him. Be smart and don't let your relationship burn out by forcing him into excessive involuntary chores.

Every morning, I drive down to the local Starbuck's and order my customary "tall drip coffee of the day with no room for cream." I pay $1.50 and usually leave a tip of ten cents, which I slam into the tip jar so it makes a loud enough sound that might get the workers to think it's a larger amount.

One day I asked a part-time employee why he liked working there. He responded, "It's a lot of fun here, and I meet tons of great-looking women." The upside aspects of having a part-time job at Starbuck's also include flexible hours, limited responsibility, and light workloads. However, working part-time means low pay and few career benefits, too.

In her love life, a woman may find that many potential love candidates are only suited for a part-time role. This may frustrate her since her return will be limited like with a part-time job at Starbuck's. Yet, trying to coerce that type of man into larger commitments and long-term planning is a difficult struggle that predictably will meet with resistance and excuses. It's better to realize that some men sign on as part-time romantic playmates, but have no intention or desire to work full-time on being your love partner.

The goal discussed in this chapter is finding the type of man who will want to take on the role of a full-time love partner along with the additional responsibilities of long-term commitments. This kind of man recognizes that there will be long-term benefits such as security, emotional support, growth, intimacy, peace of mind, and possibly a family.

SOME MEN ONLY WANT A PART-TIME ROLE

A woman sometimes has problems finding men who will offer the type of full-time commitment she's seeking. This woman will often believe that once a man truly loves her, he'll leave his old lifestyle behind and embrace an entirely new kind of life with her. After all, she would naturally do this for him.

The following example describes how one woman has been dealing with a man in her love life who only seems comfortable in a limited role:

> "I've been with my boyfriend for just over eight months. Things have been moving fairly slow, in my view. But I do tend to like to move fast in relationships. I am very happy, and I can see myself marrying this man. But the one thing that bothers me is that he doesn't call or see me as much as I would like. We only see each other once a week and he

usually calls every three days or so. By the way, he
only lives one mile away so I don't really understand
why we can't see each other more. He says it's
because he works a lot during the week and it is not
intentional. He works long days, comes home,
works out, and goes to bed. Is it too much to ask to
see him one more day a week for an hour or two?
And now he's telling me that he's got a lot of other
things going on and that he might be spending even
less time with me! Can a relationship even work
this way? I want to do what he needs me to do right
now and be patient. But I don't know how much
patience is acceptable. I have not heard from him in
about a week. I don't know why a guy can't call
just to say, 'Hi!' Is this something that will change?
Or is the relationship going nowhere fast? I think
we are perfect, so I want to give him his space and
time. But when is it okay for me to demand more?"

My response to this type of story is that a woman has to size
up her man like an employer evaluates a job applicant to see
if the person fits the available role. Certainly there are types
of careers which will be more demanding on a man's time.
Still, he should care enough to find ways to include an
important woman in his life. Generally, men who are only
willing to give a small part of their attention to a woman are
not good candidates for the role of full-time love partner.

THE FOUR KINDS OF LOVE PARTNERSHIPS

In the context of romantic relationships, here are the four
major roles that an exclusive love-partner would fall into:

⑨ **Part-Time Only.** A part-time boyfriend does his own
thing while you do yours. Sometimes this is a new couple

that's taking it slow, and other times it's a couple that does not have much in common. Being a part-time boyfriend is usually a temporary situation. Perhaps the man isn't totally into the woman yet, or possibly he'll emerge over time as a self-absorbed man with many other consuming priorities in his life. Being part-time is a type of casual dating relationship with only limited responsibilities, and a woman must be careful about determining if this is merely a relationship phase or a sign of a man's lack of interest in having more.

ꙮ **Part-Time With Exceptions.** This is a more complex situation where the man is single at heart, but has occasional periods of devoted love. A part-time boyfriend with exceptions might make grand gestures of love, be part of a long-distance romance, talk about the future in detail, and do or say other things that make the woman hopeful for a long-term partner. But this kind of guy doesn't include her in many of his plans for the future and keeps much of his life private and separate from her. This is the trickiest type of man to gauge because his sporadic romantic actions may indicate emotional desire, but at the same time he may offer little in terms of consistency or security in the relationship.

ꙮ **Full-Time Only.** Most women think this is the ideal partnership. This is where a man devotes most of his free time to the new relationship with her. This is particularly true of a man who didn't enjoy the single life, may not have any friends, and isn't sacrificing anything financially by getting more deeply involved in the love relationship. But this is the type of relationship that many other men fear most. They believe that a woman who is bent on having this will make her man give up all the things that he once enjoyed. That could mean his friends, family, sports, hobbies, and alone time. Men who have enjoyed their single life may find that this full-time love-partner situation becomes too confining and/or boring. What seems like an ideal situation at first becomes less enticing over time.

✆ **Full-Time With Exceptions.** For men with many interests, this is the ideal love situation. They are full-time committed partners at heart, but they also have time and — for lack of a better word — "permission" to do some of the things that they've always loved. It takes an enlightened woman to understand that letting go of the reins occasionally prevents resentment from building up. This also gives her man a chance to do something outside of the relationship that is both healthy and satisfying for him. A happy man will automatically reciprocate his good feelings back to the woman who understands him.

By being aware of these four love-situations, a smart woman can aim more for a "full-time love partner with exceptions" arrangement. This is the one that is most appealing to a typical man because it eases his fear of lost freedom. At the same time, the arrangement offers both partners the long-term benefits of a committed love relationship.

SMART MOVE #16: EXPAND HIS INTEREST IN YOU

Here are some ideas to help you persuade your man to go from an elusive part-time boyfriend to a satisfied full-time love partner:

☞ **Stay attractive in the same ways.** In competitive sports, there is a common phrase that says, "Go with what got you there." In a romantic-love relationship, it is equally important to retain the appeal that initially attracted the man into your life. That means continuing to take care of your appearance, being warm and receptive, and remembering to be thoughtful and considerate like you were at the beginning. Don't ever lower the standards in your relationship by taking each other for granted.

☞ **Take part in some of his interests.** It's a good idea for both partners to be able to visit the other person's world periodically. This prevents couples from living separate lives or drifting too far apart. If you show little or no interest whatsoever in his activities, you are limiting the relationship you have with each other.

☞ **Get along well with his inner circle.** Do your best to maintain good relations with your partner's friends and family. Although you may not approve of their influence on your man, you'll score more points by aligning yourself with these folks rather than confronting them. Try to avoid being the kind of woman who gets between a man and the people he likes and associates with.

☞ **Stop any high-maintenance emotional tendencies.** If it takes too much to keep a woman happy, then a man will often start building resentment towards her. A woman has to realize that it is neither natural nor healthy for a man to be forced to excessively prove his love because of her emotional insecurities. What you gain in assurances will be lost in residual animosity.

❧ **Don't let your upkeep become your downfall.** Most men are concerned about dating women who spend tons of money or require a lot of material things. While a man may appear generous in the courting stage, it's more likely that he's also gauging how much it costs to keep the woman happy with her lifestyle. A woman who convinces a man that she's sensible with her money will help alleviate his ever-present financial concerns.

❧ **Leave him alone periodically to recharge.** I once saw Jerry Seinfeld do a stand-up comedy routine where he offered women this simple piece of marital advice: *If you want to keep a man happy, leave him alone.* As funny as it sounds, it is still true in the context of making sure that a man has the right balance in his life. Typically a man will need to juggle the time he has for you, work, other people, and himself. If a man truly loves you, rest assured that this "time to recharge" will probably be short in duration and only occasional in frequency. The main thing to remember is that you will score big points by understanding his occasional need to — as John Gray, the author of *Men Are from Mars, Women Are from Venus* says — "go into his cave."

❧ **Be willing to exchange control for increased passion.** While we want 100% of a love partner's commitment to a relationship, it's not the same as demanding 100% of their time. Whatever you gain by forcing your partner to do what is not of any redeeming value, you'll end up losing in resentment. Be willing to let go of control periodically to revive the energies of your partner. By doing so, you'll have a happier partner who will naturally reciprocate this back to you in multiple positive ways.

The philosophy of expanding rather than limiting a man's interest in you and the relationship allows the opportunity for your love to grow and it benefits both partners. This also provides an inviting scenario for otherwise commitment-fearing men.

WHAT TO DO NOW

Take a moment now and think of one or two simple ways that you could expand a partner's interest in you and the relationship. Brainstorm on this whether or not you are currently seeing someone. Are there creative ways that you could help a partner to recharge his romantic batteries? Is there also something that you might do in order to make yourself healthier and more attractive physically?

Now take a moment and think of times in your past when you did things that limited a partner's interests or desires. Perhaps there were times when you didn't get along well with other people in a partner's life and that caused him to be resentful of you. Identify two or three things that limited his interest and resolve to stop getting involved in those behaviors in the future. Replace them with things that will make a man feel better about a relationship's future.

THE BOTTOM LINE

Dating sucks when you try to limit a man's life or are unable to encourage him to spend much time with you. But dating rocks when you expand his interest wisely so that you both receive the long-term benefits of emotional security, personal growth, deep intimacy, and peace of mind.

Seventeen

Relationship Challenges

DATING ROCKS WHEN YOU
HANDLE PROBLEMS EFFECTIVELY

"Serious difficulties don't vanish
by themselves, they are standing around
your bed when you open the eyes
the next morning."

Vicki Baum
Author of *I Know What I'm Worth* (1964)

189

chal•lenge: 1. a call or summons to engage in a contest, fight, or battle of strength and skill. 2. in the context of romantic relationships, the special effort needed to handle inevitable problems, obstacles, differences, or disagreements. 3. the ability to handle adversity without harming the relationship.

An honest male perspective: Problems are like weeds. They will pop up unexpectedly and attack the health of your love garden. Instead of being surprised by problems, anticipate their arrival in advance and know exactly how you're going to eliminate them.

Desperate Housewives is a prime-time soap opera that became a surprise hit. The storylines of the show take a dark look at the secret struggles of a small group of forty-something neighborhood women. Underneath the outward appearance of normal American suburbia lies the typical dissatisfaction that women confront in their real lives. Issues that the show addresses include being taken for granted by men, loneliness, divorce, infidelity, and the hazards of sticking one's nose into other people's business. This show provides a candid view of middle America that strikes a chord with large numbers of men and women alike.

Desperate Housewives certainly has created a sensational buzz. And through the program, America gets a wide open and often comical look at the kinds of relationships problems that are kept hush-hush in today's mainstream media.

For a smart woman hoping to keep the love she cherishes in her life, it is important to know how to effectively handle the challenges in the relationship. That way, she can avoid becoming an unhappy "desperate housewife" herself.

Do You Approach Your Challenges Wisely?

Problems of some variety will show up in your love relationships whether you are aware of them or not. If you handle the problems that come your way in an effective manner, they can become opportunities for learning and personal growth as well as an important test of emotional maturity. However, if you don't handle your problems well, they can have severe negative consequences. One result can be a downward spiral into relationship failure.

One woman sent me the following email about the way she has chosen to deal with a difficult challenge in her love life:

"I got sick and tired of fighting with my husband Bob about his lack of sexual drive. So what was my solution? I began an affair with a neighbor! I know it's morally wrong, but it surprisingly seems to have helped our marriage. My husband and I are fighting less and I don't get on his case about his sex drive anymore. Bob appears to be a lot happier, too. I know that men have affairs all the time in order to fulfill their sexual needs; now I find that this can work for a woman as well. I think if I can stay discreet about it that I can pull this off on a regular basis. My one fear though is getting caught and hurting my family. I really do appreciate my husband and what a great father he is to our son and daughter. This may sound strange, but I'm really not feeling any guilt at this time. Does that mean that it's okay for me to continue in this affair? Everything seems to be working perfectly now."

My reply to a woman in this type of questionable situation is simply *the ends don't justify the means!* Doing something that you know is morally wrong is never the right thing to do. Never! When faced with a challenge in life, it's always best to explore solutions that are sensible, honest, and morally sound in order to avoid results that will have negative long-term side-effects.

Ultimately, your overall approach to any adversity in your life is more important than the actual situation you face at the time. Having a reliable system in place for handling problems is what will serve you best in your lifelong quest for lasting love and fulfillment. Don't fall into the lazy habit of choosing a course of action simply because it is the quickest, easiest, or least painful route.

DON'T LET MINOR ANNOYANCES TURN MAJOR

A healthy relationship is one that offers an abundance of consistent pleasure and very little pain for both love partners. On the other hand, an unhealthy relationship is one that is filled with consistent pain and very little pleasure, and which is not likely to ever change for the better.

What gradually changes a romantic relationship from healthy to unhealthy is the buildup of resentment and the absence of positive feelings. It is important to realize that resentment can start off being just a small annoyance over something such as an insensitive remark that a man makes about a woman in jest. However, when this type of remark is made excessively and/or consistently over time, a woman can intensify her reaction to levels of major resentment.

While every relationship challenge has its own set of unique circumstances, an ongoing policy of handling problems of any variety as they surface can help keep your differences at the "minor annoyance" level. That way, you can prevent emotions from escalating into the kind of destructive resentment that eats away at the love in your relationship.

SMART MOVE #17: PREVENT RESENTMENT FROM BUILDING

Here are some helpful pointers on how to handle any kind of relationship problem that comes your way with more control and effectiveness:

☞ **See problems as temporary challenges.** The first simple step is to refer to your "problems" from now on as "challenges." The word "challenge" implies that there is a workable solution that can be found with the proper mix of courage, determination, flexibility, discipline, knowledge, and skill. Challenges tend to be temporary in nature and require higher levels of performance in order to overcome them. If a couple can rise to the occasion and muster the will to succeed, then they will eventually find a way to restore and maintain their love for each other.

☞ **Honestly admit your mistakes right away.** One way to disarm a potentially difficult situation is to admit your mistakes quickly and emphatically. That way, you will give your partner the proper assurances that this problem will be approached in a more balanced manner in the future. Do this instead of trying to wage a one-sided attack on where he's been wrong. For the time being, make sure that you let your admission of the mistake stand alone without negating its value by saying something like "What I did was wrong and I am sincerely sorry, but...." (Don't add any excuses or tell him why he's a big part of the problem.) If you try the suggested approach, your partner may likely reciprocate back by admitting his mistakes as well.

☺ **Attack the problem but not the person.** Make sure that you separate the problem from the person. You want to reinforce the idea that you love the person, but you hate their bad behaviors. Along the same lines, never question the other person's intent and don't attack their character if you want to prevent an escalation of ill will. When dealing with men, realize that they sometimes do and say dumb things simply because they don't attach much significance to a particular action or its consequences. This is in contrast to how the typical woman would probably view it. If a playful guy thinks that something is no big deal, you can expect him to do or say almost anything.

☺ **Can you handle the truth?** People often claim that they want to hear the absolute truth. However, can they really accept it without getting their feelings hurt? As a communicator, one tactful way of presenting a hard truth is to spend a lot of time explaining the nature of what is about to be said. That way, the intent of the message is less likely to be misconstrued. So establish the nature of a difficult discussion, get permission to share the details, and then freely state your truth. A wise communicator will also follow up their statements with a reminder of why honesty is essential for the long-term health of any love relationship. Interestingly, how well people handle the truth creates a precedent on whether truths will be shared or omitted in the future. If you discover that a partner has been telling you a pack of lies, understand that part of the problem may be his perception that you can't handle the truth. In any case, people should know that it's best to stick with honesty. My feeling is that if the truth will destroy a relationship, so be it. Actually, the strange thing I've discovered is that the truth seldom blows up a relationship — instead what is almost guaranteed to destroy the love connection is avoiding the truth, better known as lying or lying by omission.

℗ **Don't be too negative.** While it's true that most problems are negative in nature, it doesn't mean that we can't find some positive value in the process of overcoming them. Remind yourself that while there may be problems or imperfections in your relationship, there are still plenty of other things to be grateful about, too. In addition, discipline your thinking so that you clearly define your challenge and not make it appear worse than it actually is. The most important point here is that negative problems are handled best when you are in the most positive and constructive frame of mind.

℗ **Focus on workable solutions.** Put an immediate end to the pointless rehashing of a problem and move forward by focusing on workable solutions. By doing this, you will think about constructive responses rather than waste more time dwelling on what has already happened and can't be changed. The object here is to come up with a wide range of possible solutions for your particular relationship challenge and mutually decide on the best course of action to pursue. Put your energy where you'll get the best results and that's by focusing on the best solutions and creating a goal-achieving plan of actions.

☺ **What is the larger objective?** If you can ask this question throughout the process of solving your relationship challenge, you will be able to keep your discussion on purpose. The larger objective may include such things as: (1) making sure that you don't take each other for granted, (2) improving communication, (3) learning more about your partner's beliefs about your relationship, and (4) learning how to grow as a couple, to name a few. The larger objective is always positive and is meant to bring happiness and fulfillment to both partners. In the heat of your battles, always come back to the larger objective so that you'll be reminded of how you will both benefit.

☺ **Get professional help or get out.** If you find that the weight of your problems becomes too heavy for you to handle, seek high-quality professional counseling. This may require getting help for yourself first and later getting help for your partner as well. Select a counselor who has a good track record for success and is naturally appealing to both partners. Still, sometimes we find that despite all of our efforts to repair the serious problems in a relationship, we fail to observe one or more of the following: (1) a willingness to seek any kind of help, (2) a willingness to be responsible, (3) a willingness to forgive, (4) a willingness to love, or (5) a willingness to even try. At that point, it's clearly time to get out.

You will arrive at your love destiny as a result of all of the choices that you make over time. Increase your chances for success by having a sensible and reliable system in place for handling your relationship challenges. That way, you can avoid unnecessarily harsh clashes and prevent hard feelings from destroying your love.

WHAT TO DO NOW

Take a moment to think of a time when a relationship challenge surprised you in the past. If you can't think of one, use an example from the life of a friend or family member. In the example you've chosen, in what ways did you or the other person react? Now look at the same example again. From the points raised in this chapter's discussion, come up with more than one resourceful new approach to the problem. Can you see the positive differences that could be made by choosing new more empowering responses?

Make a resolution now regarding the next time you are surprised by an immediate challenge. Commit to staying clear of knee-jerk reactions and instead call for a quick time-out. For example, excuse yourself to go to the restroom to freshen up. Once there, gather yourself emotionally. And when you're ready, return to face your challenge equipped with a more resourceful state of mind and an eagerness to demonstrate your improved emotional maturity.

THE BOTTOM LINE

Dating sucks when problems crop up repeatedly in your love life and send you into an emotional tailspin. But dating rocks when you can anticipate and handle every kind of challenging situation with wisdom, maturity, control, and love.

Eighteen

Anger Management
DATING SUCKS WHEN YOU CAN'T CONTROL YOUR UPSETS

"Resentment is an evil so costly
to our peace that we should find it
cheap to forgive."

Hannah More
English poet and playwright (1745-1835)

an•ger: 1. a strong feeling of displeasure aroused by being unjustly wronged or injured. 2. when someone violates your most important rules for proper behavior. 3. in the context of dating, what every smart woman or man must control in order to prevent ill feelings from destroying their chances for lasting love.

An honest male perspective: Almost all upsets are externally triggered, but internally driven. So it's not what happens to you that matters, it's how you choose to respond that is important.

In November 2004, the National Basketball Association witnessed the worst player-fan brawl in its 59-year history. For ten minutes, chaos reigned at the Palace of Auburn Hills, which is the Detroit Pistons' home court. Angry players from the visiting Indiana Pacers went into the stands to punch unruly fans, who escalated the melee by throwing popcorn, ice, folding chairs, etc., at the players.

As Larry Brown, the veteran coach of the hometown Detroit Pistons said, "It's the ugliest thing that I've seen in all of my years as a coach or player."

As a result of this brawl, a team member from the Indiana Pacers, Ron Artest, was suspended for the remainder of the season. This suspension cost Artest over $5 million in salary for his role as one of the main instigators. Reportedly Artest went into the stands after a beer-throwing fan who was reacting to a confrontation between the Pacer player and the

Pistons' Ben Wallace. Artest had fouled Wallace, and Wallace is said to have reacted by hitting Artest in the throat with both palms. The fan's full beer then hit Ron Artest square in the face. If Artest had been able to control his anger at that point, he could have saved himself a lot of money and spared the league this embarrassing and nearly tragic event.

Whenever an individual loses control of their temper, the resulting actions can become both dangerous and regrettable. This is true in professional basketball as well as in a relationship with someone you are dating.

> "Beware of anger. It is the most difficult to remove of all the hindrances. But it is the alcohol of the body, you know, and the devil of it is that it deadens the perceptions."
> Margery Allingham
> Author of *The Tiger in the Smoke* (1952)

The simple fact is that we can choose to be responsible for our actions by having a controlled response to an upset or we can let our emotions spur our reaction. If we get carried away and over-react, it often causes us to suffer negative and sometime life-altering consequences.

WILL YOU RESPOND OR WILL YOU REACT?

Getting upset recklessly with a partner will build resentment and create doubt in the relationship. One woman emailed me the following example regarding how her frequent upsets nearly destroyed her love life:

> "My boyfriend and I went through a period where I seemed to be constantly upset with him. We'd be

fine for a few days and then I would get moody. It was always about the same thing — my desire for more physical intimacy. My boyfriend felt that he was giving as much as he could and that I didn't appreciate the moments that we had. I finally made a public scene in front of our friends. I yelled at him for not showing me enough love. He was thinking that I'm too high maintenance, and I was thinking that he doesn't appreciate me. But after a week off from each other, I realized that he has always been emotionally supportive. I was just being too needy, too demanding, and too emotional. I came real close to losing him because I was expecting him to show me love like a woman does and didn't realize that he's doing it in the way that feels natural to him."

Once you fully realize how destructive outbursts can be to a relationship and your emotional well-being, you'll take the necessary steps to regain your sense of control. It's much wiser to respond intelligently than to react recklessly in any part of your life. This will help you prevent an accumulation of resentment that could tip the scales on the side of failure instead of success in your relationship.

BREAK THE PATTERN BUT NOT YOUR NOSE!

One time I tried to break up a heated argument between two women in Hennessey's Bar and Grill in Seal Beach, California. My intention was to break their behavioral pattern with something called a "pattern interrupt," which I learned from the advanced communication seminars that I had attended over the years.

In the heat of their argument, I stepped between the two women and said, "It's time for you girls to get naked!"

Unfortunately, one of them — a tough Australian blonde — took instant offense to my remark and punched me in the face. I ended up on the floor with a bloody nose and a stunned look on my face. A crowd gathered to see what all the commotion was about, resulting in laughter aimed at me and my foolish comment. The woman who hit me apologized later, but advised me not to talk that way to a lady.

While my nose hurt as much as my bruised male ego, the "pattern interrupt" I used stopped the argument from escalating. In this case, the two women not only ended their fighting, but they both got a good laugh at a common enemy — me.

SMART MOVE #18: MANAGE YOUR UPSETS

When we get upset, it's easy to do or say unwise and regrettable things. Therefore, it is important that we learn how to control our upsets so that we can stop contributing ill feelings to our relationships.

The following are questions to help you get a better handle on your emotions whenever adversity or stress causes you to want to lash back unwisely:

☺ **How small is this act in the grand scheme of life?** A cardiologist was once asked for his advice for reducing the stress that leads to strokes and heart attacks. He replied, "Rule #1: Don't sweat the small stuff. Rule #2: It's all small stuff." We often have to be reminded about how small our personal worries can be in comparison to the bigger issues of life. At the same time, realize that life is too short to be wasting your major energies on minor issues. Whenever you're faced with a potential argument, shrink it down to size by contrasting it with the more important issues of your life.

⚕ **Will this really matter much a year from now?** What seems significant in the moment may in fact be minor in retrospect. If you move ahead in time and look back on today, you may be able to regain your perspective on the current issue. You could find that once again you're faced with a situation where you have put too much emotion on too minor a subject. By adding the time perspective of one year, you may be able to shrink the intensity of the current issue under debate.

⚕ **What have you respected, liked, trusted, or admired about this person in the past?** Sometimes you have to be reminded of what is great about the person you're dealing with. That way, you can realize that they're not all bad, and might even be wonderful. We're all guilty of doing or saying stupid things. It's smart to give those we've appreciated in the past an occasional break for minor screw-ups.

⚕ **Was this act really intended to harm you?** If you want to protect yourself from the actions and opinions of others, realize this fact immediately: *People do things first and foremost for their own benefit.* Also understand that what's important or real to you may not be the same for someone else. Therefore, expect people to choose the quickest, easiest, or least painful pathway in order to gain pleasure or avoid pain. Rarely is an act intentionally meant to harm another person. It could just be that there is some kind of benefit for the one who is behind it. Remember that in almost all cases, men have no intentions of causing a woman they love any kind of real suffering.

☺ **Does this kind of thing happen all of the time?** Repeated intentional acts of meanness should be promptly reprimanded, but an occasional mess-up should be given a temporary pass. Even when things do happen repeatedly, it may still be wise to refrain from saying the trigger phrase, "You always do that!" If you want to prevent your disagreements from escalating out of control, be sure to measure the frequency of an unpleasant act accurately.

☺ **What is the other side of the story?** There's a saying that goes, "No matter how thin you slice it, there are always two sides." In order to handle any kind of problem, it's important to gather all of the facts first. That way, you can acquire an understanding of the other side of the conflict. If you can't find that opposing perspective, delay your judgments and avoid jumping to conclusions. Hear out the other person so that you have a chance to evaluate the situation with more precision and respond in ways that demonstrate your increasing emotional maturity.

☺ **How could this act be appropriate or even useful?** As wise and caring adults, we shouldn't react or respond hostilely when someone's actions are not intentional, excessive, and inappropriate for the situation at hand. And if we can see a long-term benefit from a short-term setback, we are able to convert the negatives we receive into positives. When there is indeed a real problem related to their actions, just make your perspective and needs clear to them in a cooperative manner.

☺ **How can you vent the anger in a more constructive way?** Emotional upsets are stored in our physical bodies where they can linger and destroy our health. We can release this damaging physical and emotional tension constructively by exercising or talking with a caring friend. The alternative is to vent your anger in unhealthy ways like drinking alcohol, overeating, or verbally bashing others. A better way to handle your upsets is to change your mental focus by doing something that you enjoy like shopping, reading, or watching a movie. Another way to vent is to delay your reactions until cooler heads can prevail. Realize that you have many choices to release your tensions, some of which are healthier for you than others. By being in a better state of mind and body, you'll handle your challenges with other people more effectively.

☺ **What could be funny about this?** A creative alternative for handling upsets is to find the humor in an otherwise serious situation. If you're really good at this, you accomplish three vital things: (1) you break your pattern of physiology by putting a smile on your face and a spark of joy in your eyes, (2) you change your voice tones and breathing patterns by laughing out loud, and (3) you change the words you use by referring to the situation from that point forward as being either funny, ridiculous, outrageous, hilarious, silly, or stupid. One trick that I often use when faced with a tough challenge is to ask out loud, "Am I on freaking *Candid Camera* or what?"

By managing your upsets, you'll be able to prevent resentment from eating away at the love that you've worked so hard to enjoy. This process begins with a firm commitment on your part to respond in an emotionally mature manner instead of reacting foolishly.

WHAT TO DO NOW

Think back on a time when you completely lost your temper and then later knew that you shouldn't have. In this situation, refer to the previous discussion and find one question that would have stopped you from responding so unwisely. Resolve that the next time you feel the heat of anger swelling up within you, you'll break your pattern of reaction by asking yourself out loud, "What question do I need to ask myself right now in order to take immediate control of this challenging situation?"

> "Their anger dug out for itself a deep channel,
> so that future anger might more easily flow."
> Radclyffe Hall
> Author of *The Well of Loneliness* (1928)

Remember, asking the right questions will steer you away from unwise knee-jerk reactions and towards the kind of elegant responses that build rapport, demonstrate emotional maturity, and restore faith in the future of all your interpersonal relationships.

THE BOTTOM LINE

Dating sucks when you have no control of your negative emotions and you gradually destroy the things you cherish so much in your love life. But dating rocks when you get a firm grip on your upsets and grow as a person who is deserving of respect, admiration, trust, and love.

Nineteen

The Certainty Principle

DATING ROCKS WHEN YOU CREATE CONVICTIONS OF THE HEART

"Men like frivolity – before marriage;
but they demand all the sterner
virtues afterwards."

Nellie McClung
Canadian writer (1873-1951)

cer•tain•ty: 1. freedom from doubt and having supreme confidence. 2. an absolute knowing that something is fact, unquestionable, and indisputable. 3. in the context of love, when both partners put their full trust into their relationship because of their unshakable convictions of the heart.

An honest male perspective: For passionate, romantic people, getting attracted to someone and falling in love is fun and easy. However, the harder part for these people is staying in love by making the relationship work. While all of that process may not seem like fun, the challenge of making a relationship work is the time-tested path to happiness and fulfillment. In previous chapters, we've covered various ways to prevent negative feelings from destroying a relationship. This chapter will focus on what it takes to create continuous positive memories that accumulate value for the love partnership.

Britney Spears was recognized by *Access Hollywood* as the most-covered celebrity of 2004. With two quick marriages within that year — the first to a high-school classmate from Louisiana (this union ended in an annulment) and second to one of her backup dancers — the Pop Princess certainly kept her love life in the entertainment headlines.

Britney's second marriage, to backup dancer Kevin Federline, was reportedly scheduled originally for November 2004. However, the two moved the date up to September 19, and wed in a top-secret ceremony in the backyard of a private residence, despite not having filed their marriage license yet.

"I know we're not completely legal until we file the license," Spears said. "But in a real sense, in a spiritual sense, we're married. I believe you also marry in your heart and that means much more than a piece of paper....the real truth is love. We know we have that."

A wedding comes at a time when both people feel that they are deeply in love with each other. At this early point, the future appears filled with ever-lasting happiness. But with national statistics stating that one out of two marriages ends in divorce, the reality is that love as we've come to know it doesn't last for many couples.

As a smart woman looking to get and keep a long-term love relationship, it's important to know what actions to take and which ones to avoid. Otherwise, the love that you thought was the "real truth" may turn out to be just another failure to add to the national divorce statistics.

LOVE DOESN'T LAST AUTOMATICALLY

A love that doesn't last can be a frustrating, hurtful, and disappointing experience for both partners. One woman sent the following note to me about how her once-great relationship eventually turned sour:

> "I'm writing to you because I'm convinced that love doesn't last! In my situation, I really loved my boyfriend up until recently and I thought that he was my true soulmate. But that's certainly not how I feel anymore! Nobody knows what I have had to put up with when it comes to him. He lies all the time, gets jealous for no apparent reason, and hangs

> out with his buddies every chance he gets. What really ticks me off is that he's always checking out the hot women during every date we have! He almost never makes any plans for us. And when he finally does, he's usually real late, cancels at the last moment, or has some lame excuse about being too tired. Of course, when it comes to romance and making love tenderly, I get very little. This man claims he loves me so much that he can't live without me, but he avoids making any real efforts to be sensitive to my needs. I think that I've finally had enough of this miserable relationship. It keeps getting worse, not better! But what's bad is that I don't see how it could ever change. I'm out of here!"

While good fortune plays an important part in experiencing the magical qualities of a romantic relationship, long-term adult love requires more hard work and emotional maturity than mere luck. For many young couples, the concept of work seems like a sure-fire way of killing the romance. But as more enlightened people will attest, keeping your fingers crossed and hoping things will always be great is not a proactive, sensible strategy for love. Instead, you'll need to learn to handle the inevitable challenges that will occur in your relationship over time.

CERTAINTY STARTS THE FLOW OF LOVE

As a former member of motivational expert Tony Robbins' seminar trainer staff, I was introduced to several methods for achieving success in various areas of a person's life. I remember sitting in a hotel conference room in Palm Springs, California back in the mid-1990s when Robbins came into our trainer's meeting talking a mile a minute. His topic was a new understanding that he had around the concept of beliefs. Tony said in effect that the most critical key to becoming successful at anything of value was for a person to possess a "flat-out knowing" or "100% conviction" about their ability to achieve a desired outcome. He eventually labeled this concept "absolute certainty."

I've found that the certainty principle can also be applied to love. My major point here is that being completely certain about your love for each other is what will enable you and your partner to love and give freely without hesitation. When certainty is present, couples will do all they can to prevent negative feelings from persisting. In addition, they do everything in their power to experience an abundance of positive feelings for each other.

Conviction is the highest form of belief. With daily random acts of warmth, kindness, patience, and love, a couple can block out a lot of the negative feelings that put an end to many relationships. These acts allow each person to experience the peace of mind that comes from true convictions reinforced by visible actions.

SMART MOVE #19: CREATE UNSHAKABLE CONVICTIONS

A basic strategy for keeping love alive is to: (1) prevent all negative feelings from stacking up and (2) make sure that a wide array of highly positive feelings accumulate abundantly. When this becomes a consistent pattern, then both people become absolutely certain that their love will last and bring each other joy.

The following are ideas on how to establish the conviction that causes couples to give abundantly to their partner so the relationship will be enhanced:

⊚ **Use loving words, gestures, and actions.** Give sincere appreciation to your mate by what you say and do. While conventional wisdom says that actions speak louder than words, make sure that you don't let your actions do all of the talking either. Well-chosen words and thoughtful small acts can often strike a deeper chord with your partner than an infrequent grand gesture of love.

⊚ **Fill each other's needs.** Do your best to give in a variety of different ways to your partner. There will be times when an act of kindness will be more greatly appreciated than an act of passion. Your mate may be in a place where he needs to feel more connected or understood than at other times. The key is to be the one who fills your partner's most sensitive needs in a style that is uniquely you. Otherwise, a lack of sensitivity may cause an unenlightened love partner to go outside of the relationship in order to have his emotional needs filled by someone else. This can lead to negative consequences for both of you.

⊚ **Ask for what you want.** Your partner is not a mind reader. If you're not getting your emotional needs filled, you'll have to ask for his assistance. However, asking must be done correctly or else it will be construed as you just being demanding. To help you ask more intelligently, here are some key things to consider: (1) ask at an appropriate time, (2) ask for permission to ask, (3) ask specifically for what you want, (4) ask by stating what's in it for him, (5) ask in a sensitive, loving way, (6) ask with a higher purpose in mind, and (7) ask with the courage and conviction of knowing that this is the right thing to do. Think of asking for what you want as a form of feedback that is necessary in order to keep your relationship correctly on track towards excellence.

֎ **Choose love over being right.** Often in our relationships, we become fixated on what's wrong or needs to be improved. Sometimes we even withhold our love until certain conditions are met by our partners. But most importantly, we must realize that our basic love for each other can be lost in the daily struggle over small issues. When we begin to understand that this destructive habit is occurring, it's important to choose the higher value of love (kindness, caring, trust, patience) over the lower value of being right or getting your way on insignificant things.

֎ **Never break the trust.** Some people believe that they have to go outside of their relationship in order to have their emotional needs filled. This may be appropriate in some cases, but clear boundaries must be drawn. If these needs involve some sort of immoral behavior, like having an affair, then feelings of betrayal may completely destroy the relationship. It's often too late and not enough to apologize after the fact. A wise partner realizes that trust is like tissue in the wind; once torn it can never be returned to its original pristine state. Always remember that destroying trust is a relationship deal-breaker for many people.

֎ **Don't ever threaten the relationship.** When things go wrong in a love relationship, it's a common but unwise practice to threaten to leave your partner. We tend to

Your Maturity Checklist

IDENTIFY YOUR AREAS FOR SELF-IMPROVEMENT

• Keep your commitments	Poor	Fair	Good
• Deal effectively with uncertainty	Poor	Fair	Good
• Sensitive to the needs of others	Poor	Fair	Good
• Eager to take on new tasks	Poor	Fair	Good
• Finish what you start	Poor	Fair	Good
• Cope with difficult people	Poor	Fair	Good
• Tell the truth, don't lie	Poor	Fair	Good
• Respect the rights of other people	Poor	Fair	Good
• Take responsibility for your actions	Poor	Fair	Good
• Manage your upsets and anger	Poor	Fair	Good
• Willingness to discuss your feelings	Poor	Fair	Good
• Recognize and deal with your fears	Poor	Fair	Good
• Earn the rightful respect of others	Poor	Fair	Good
• Cope with frustration and failure	Poor	Fair	Good
• Acknowledge your limitations	Poor	Fair	Good
• Share attention with others	Poor	Fair	Good
• Show sincere interest in others	Poor	Fair	Good
• Display competence and skill	Poor	Fair	Good
• Motivated to work hard to succeed	Poor	Fair	Good
• Save money and invest	Poor	Fair	Good
• Show self-control over impulses	Poor	Fair	Good
• Sort out fact from fiction	Poor	Fair	Good
• Resist negative peer-pressure	Poor	Fair	Good
• Honor your parents and elders	Poor	Fair	Good
• Reciprocate kind acts from others	Poor	Fair	Good
• Relate well to both genders, all ages	Poor	Fair	Good
• Behave in sincere, genuine ways	Poor	Fair	Good
• Flexible under changing conditions	Poor	Fair	Good
• Have patience and remain poised	Poor	Fair	Good

THE BOTTOM LINE

Increase your level of emotional maturity so that you get to keep the love that you've attained. Otherwise, relationships are going to be a constant source of pain for you, regardless of how strong your mutual romantic chemistry was initially.

think that if something is not working to our satisfaction, then someone is to blame. At that point, we then will typically place the blame on the other person without enough regard for our own contributions to the problem. If creating fear in a partner doesn't get them to change to our liking, we can be tempted to look elsewhere towards greener pastures. A wiser choice is to discipline your thinking in this area. Creating uncertainty in a relationship is a guaranteed way of stopping the flow of love. Once this happens, a downward spiral of resentment and poor communications leads to regrettable actions and irreversible negative consequences.

⊛ **Schedule and create special moments to treasure.** Smart life-management strategies include making sure that you and your partner have enough quality time together. You can prevent neglect from ruining your romance by scheduling regular date nights, weekend getaways, and memorable vacations throughout the year. These special moments together can revitalize your love for each other. In addition, be on the lookout for romantic opportunities in your normal day-to-day life which can be made extra special with a little awareness and creativity.

⊛ **Agree on a higher standard for your relationship.** If you give your relationship a fine reputation to live up to in your daily lives together, that standard will pull you through many challenging times. While others around you may accept their substandard, mediocre relationships, you and your partner can take ownership of the situation and say something like, "This challenge isn't really about us. We have come too far together to let this obstacle stand in our way. Our relationship is above all of this junk. Together, we will find a way to get through this thing. Every challenge presents us with the seeds of opportunity to grow together and become more emotionally mature." By maintaining a high standard for your relationship, you can rise above the petty bickering and deal effectively with the issues that really matter.

⑨ **Become full-time love partners with exceptions:** In Chapter 16, I wrote about the concept of full-time and part-time love partners. In most cases, the type of relationship that offers full commitment and the freedom to grow in other healthy areas is what I call "full-time partners with exceptions." In this arrangement, the two love-partners share the heart of a couple, but allow space for each person to pursue key individual interests. The amount of the exception is what has to be agreed upon between the two people in the relationship. What seems to happen frequently is that the woman will feel she is a "full-time partner only" and that her man is not contributing at the same level of commitment. This probably means that the man has to cut down on his amount of exceptions and convince his partner that his heart is fully committed to her. She, on the other hand, should become less dependent and branch out on her own in a few areas that are of particular value and interest to her. Keep in mind that a woman who appears too needy and dependent is not appreciated or desired by the overwhelming majority of men.

By creating unshakable convictions of the heart, a couple can remove any doubt about the future and create a steady flow of love that reenergizes the relationship.

WHAT TO DO NOW

If you're in a relationship right now, take a moment and decide on one thing that you can do today to increase your partner's certainty about your love for each other. It doesn't have to be a grand gesture of love. Even a simple phone call or an act of kindness like a sincere compliment would fit the bill. Just for today, be willing to raise the standards in your love life with at least one purposeful action.

If you're not currently in a relationship, think of something that you can do today to cheer up a friend, co-worker, or family member. No matter what kind of relationship you're in, remember that most of the people you associate with will respond favorably to anything that you do or say with kindness, thoughtfulness, and sincerity.

Finally, realize that you have the power to either start or stop the flow of love in your love life in a heartbeat. If your acts of love and kindness are genuine, then your partner will reciprocate back to you naturally. This simple practice will automatically reshape your love destiny together one joyful moment at a time.

THE BOTTOM LINE

Dating sucks when couples create doubt in each other and the relationship by expressing careless remarks and making unwise decisions. But dating rocks when both love partners are completely certain about their love for each other and show it through their consistent daily actions. Then they will anticipate their future together with growing enthusiasm.

Twenty

Automatic Excellence

LOVE ROCKS WHEN YOU MAINTAIN
AN ATTITUDE OF GRATITUDE

"Young love is a flame, often very hot
and fierce but still only light and
flickering. The love of the older and
disciplined heart is as coals
deep-burning, unquenchable."

Henry Ward Beecher
American social reformer (1813-1887)

ex•cel•lence: 1. reaching the state of superiority or outstanding quality or merit. 2. in the context of romantic relationships, when each partner receives tons of pleasure and value consistently and across many areas. 3. what every man and woman wants to experience in their love life forever.

An honest male perspective: Love starts to go downhill when one of the partners doesn't feel as important to the other person as before. By consistently focusing too heavily on things outside of our primary relationship, we plant the seeds of doubt in our partners. The solution lies in finding simple, everyday ways to reinforce your partner's importance to you. Use your creativity to find unique and abundant ways of demonstrating appreciation for your partner. In order to keep your relationship at a high level of excellence, a couple must make each other feel important every chance they can.

Do you remember receiving your report-card back in grade school? When I went to Ridgecrest Intermediate School in Rancho Palos Verdes, California, we were graded on basic subjects like English, social studies, math, science, foreign language, and physical education. Although I was regarded as a very smart kid, I never did receive the ultimate recognition of being a "straight A student."

The grading system back then was pretty much the same as it is now. If you receive an "A," it stood for "excellent." If you didn't do as well, then you would cither rcccive a grade of "B" for "above average," a "C" for "average," a "D" for "below average," or an "F" for "failure."

The report card was meant to let your parents know how well you were doing in school. But I remember that poor grades on a report card were also used as a warning that you might not make it to college. Hence, the poor grades were also a threat that you would never become a success in life.

YOUR RELATIONSHIP REPORT CARD

If there were such a thing as a report card for relationships, what would be the basic subjects and what kind of grades would you receive?

After tossing around this idea with some people, I came up with the following subjects for individuals in relationships to be "graded" on:

☻ **Communication:** Speaks clearly, listens attentively, and understands the partner caringly.

☻ **Chemistry:** Works on securing and maintaining a strong physical attraction and healthy sex life.

☻ **Compatibility:** Pays attention to having a lot in common in regards to lifestyle, interests, and goals.

☻ **Caring:** Acts with consistent warmth, patience, and kindness towards each other.

☻ **Commitment:** Makes and keeps sincere promises of responsibility towards the relationship.

☻ **Conflict Resolution:** Handles anger, upsets, and disagreements with effectiveness and respect.

☻ **Growth:** Is involved in a never-ending search for new areas of common interest for the future.

◈ **Trust:** Deals honestly and faithfully with each other throughout the relationship.

Being graded on these subjects would give a person a general idea of how well they are working on the relationship. And like school subjects, your own performance in a relationship can be greatly improved if you study and practice what you need to know in order to do well.

How To Get "Straight A's" In Your Relationship

In your school days, you could achieve short-term success by "cramming" for your final grades with a last-minute push of massive energy and single-minded focus. But in romantic relationships, a person needs to have a steady inner pull of enlightened short-term and long-term motivation.

Most relationships begin to fail when each partner starts to take the other one for granted. They both begin to do less for their partner and gradually give the impression that they care less about the relationship than before.

One woman gave me the following example of how she's starting to fail in her love relationship:

> "I'm really starting to resent my husband and now I'm afraid that our once-great marriage is finally falling apart. We've been married for over seven years now. When we first met, I told him that I was a modern kind of woman with high material standards. For example, I told him many years ago that I wanted a new washer and dryer. When our second child came along, I told him that we needed a bigger house. Our second child is four years old now and my husband has done absolutely nothing to make

our lives any more comfortable — no new washer, no new dryer, and no new house! About a year ago, I told him we needed an interior paint job and new carpeting for the house. He finally agreed to the paint job, but I'm still haggling with him over the new carpet. I can go on and on about all of the other things that my husband has let me down on. I'm feeling really lost at the moment. I used to be so in love with my husband, but now I'm really starting to resent him more and more as time goes by. Can you help me figure this all out before it's too late?"

If you want to get "straight A's" in your love-life, the natural way to do so is to care about the relationship by remaining grateful to your partner. We demonstrate our gratitude best by reminding ourselves daily about what we appreciate in our relationship. When we show our partners consistent sincere appreciation, it keeps our love revitalized. Therefore, with an unlimited reservoir of gratitude, we can automatically maintain the love we so deeply cherish.

Smart Move #20: Maintain An Attitude of Gratitude

Here are some important reminders to help you keep a steady flow of gratitude in your love life:

☺ **Be the first one to give.** Sometimes we feel inclined to wait for the other person to do something good for us before we reciprocate back in a similar manner. The more enlightened approach is to initiate the process of giving and receiving by being the one to give first. Don't let an opportunity to make another person's day special slip away. Be proactive in your life by adding value first.

"Gratitude unlocks the
fullness of life. It turns what
we have into enough, and
more. It turns denial into
acceptance, chaos to order,
confusion to clarity. It can
turn a meal into a feast,
a house into a home,
a stranger into a friend.
Gratitude makes sense of
our past, brings peace for
today, and creates a vision
for tomorrow."

Melody Beattie
Author of *Codependent No More* (1986)

◎ **Don't overlook the small things.** A Greek proverb reads, "Nothing will content him who is not content with a little." When we notice and appreciate the little things in life, we can make every day something special to anticipate and cherish. Take the time at the end of each day to be grateful for any small acts of kindness, brief moments of thoughtfulness, and simple things of beauty. That way, your heart will always be open to give and receive love.

◎ **Remember that things could be a lot worse.** We can experience more joy in life if we allow ourselves to recognize how good things really are. Sometimes it is useful to remind yourself how much worse your current circumstances could be. But unfortunately, most people only use the power of contrast to make themselves unhappy about how much better things "should" be. Remember that not being happy usually means that you're not being grateful.

◎ **Appreciate what really matters.** We commonly make the mistake of wasting major emotions on relatively minor things. Instead, we should enjoy more of our success and happiness and less of the things that aren't quite perfect yet. When we value our good health, the people we love, the accomplishments we're proud of, the new activities we're excited about, and what makes us happy, we remind ourselves of those things of which we are most grateful. That way, we can save our heart and soul for the things that truly matter in our lives.

◎ **Treasure all of your moments.** Some memories in our past are better than anything we will ever experience in that realm again. The past — with all of its rewards, foolishness, pleasures, and punishments — are with each of us forever. With the proper attitude, we can let the past furnish us with deep roots that can support us through the toughest of times. When we treasure our moments, the memories give us the strength and inspiration to live our lives more fully.

(*) **Gratitude makes you a better person.** When you live by a philosophy of "living is giving," you become a valuable person to society. You also become recognized as someone of value who deserves to be appreciated and trusted. Some people operate by the mistaken belief that the more you take from others, the more you have. But more enlightened souls fully realize that the more you give to others, the more you receive back for yourself. One of the biggest payoffs a person can receive by being a giver of love, warmth, and kindness is the gift of becoming a more loving person. This is something that you can take with you throughout the rest of your life regardless of how your circumstances — romantic or otherwise — change in time.

(*) **Give thanks to the heavens.** Gratitude brings peace of mind to the soul. Whenever we feel overly anxious, afraid, lonely, or unhappy in our love relationships, we've made the mistake of losing perspective on the gift of life that our Higher Power has given us. Experiencing both pain and pleasure in our relationships is all part of our remarkable journey in this world. Our gratitude is simply an acknowledgment that we appreciate the privilege to be here in the first place.

In a day and age when nothing seems to be enough, a sense of gratitude is what makes a small thing seem significant and an occasional act of love more than satisfying. By maintaining an unlimited reserve of gratitude, you can automatically keep your relationship at its highest standard for long-term success and happiness.

WHAT TO DO NOW

Think for a moment about a time when someone did something nice for you. That person may have bought you something, said kind words to you, or even provided a helping hand in a state of emergency. If that person happened to be a stranger, their actions were probably much more noticeable to you because the thoughtfulness was unexpected.

Now think of your most intimate relationships in the past or present. Have the people you loved done similar acts showing kindness, gratitude, and/or generosity? Did you acknowledge them or not?

Realize that every relationship offers plenty of chances to show our sincere appreciation for the other person. All we have to do is seize the opportunity to be thankful, generate more love, and create more joy in everyone's life.

THE BOTTOM LINE

Love sucks when you lose your appreciation for each other and fail by not giving it your all. But love rocks when you maintain your gratitude for each other on a daily basis with simple and creative acts of kindness, warmth, thoughtfulness, sensitivity, and joy.

Twenty-One

Loving Is Living

LIFE ROCKS WHEN YOU GIVE
WITH ALL OF YOUR HEART

"Someone once asked me what I regard
as the three most important require-
ments for happiness. My answer was:
A feeling that you have been honest
with yourself and those around you;
a feeling that you have done the best you
could both in your personal life and in
your work; and the ability to love others."

Eleanor Roosevelt
American first lady and writer (1884-1962)

liv•ing: 1. full of passion, interest, and vitality. 2. having love, success, happiness, and health, as well as wealth in both human and financial terms. 3. what every person receives when they give their heart and soul to themselves and others.

An honest male perspective: When you come to the end of the game, make sure that it showed that you played — got passionately involved and gave it your all. You don't want to get stuck having to explain why you never put yourself into the game.

Recent times have given a financial windfall to those who have invested wisely in real estate. If there was a poster boy for this lucrative period, my vote would certainly go for New York City's Donald Trump. Beyond Trump's real estate dealings, his name can be seen almost everywhere in the media from major corporate sponsorships, hit television reality-shows, best-selling books, mega-wealth seminars, and headline tabloid news. It's easy to think that this man and his luxurious lifestyle are the epitome of the American dream.

The pursuit of money, achievement, recognition, and power are all aimed at satisfying our basic human need to feel important and significant. In many instances, people feel that if they are notable enough, then they'll earn the love and respect of other people. But the feeling of importance in the eyes of others is almost impossible to maintain over time. In order to stay significant to others, a person must create an endless supply of newer and grander achievements as the memory of past glories fades away quickly.

Love, on the other hand, is an emotion that can grow stronger over the years in those who treasure us for who we really are. The wisdom of the ages tells us that it is the attainment of love, and not the achievement of importance, that leads us down the enlightened path to life-long happiness and fulfillment.

THE REAL LIFE OF AN AMERICAN PRESIDENT

In June 2004, our country saw the passing of its 40th President, Ronald Reagan. Here was a man who was once the most powerful person in the world. His list of achievements while in office included ending the Iranian hostage crisis, overhauling the income tax code, eliminating Soviet intermediate-range missiles, and presiding over the country's longest recorded period of peacetime prosperity without recession or depression.

But this great and powerful man was not only remembered in the eulogy for his achievements, but also for the love he had for his wife through the following words: "In a life of good fortune, he valued above all the gracious gift of his beloved wife, Nancy. During his career, Ronald Reagan passed through a thousand crowded places; but there was only one person, he said, who could make him lonely by just leaving the room."

While success and achievement are worthwhile and necessary goals in the prime earning years of our lives, they are not the ultimate source of life-long fulfillment. In whatever pursuits you choose in life, make sure that you never lose sight of what is most essential to filling up your heart and enriching your soul.

SIX MAJOR REASONS TO LIVE A LIFE OF LOVE

Here are some of the key benefits that you will receive by living your life based on giving and receiving love:

🌱 **You'll find an appropriate place to share and develop your personal gifts.** True living is more about giving of yourself than getting things from others. It is the act of giving that reveals what kind of person we are inside. The opportunity to give is the chance to share our personal gifts of character and heart in a special way that is dearly appreciated by others and is richly rewarding to ourselves.

🌱 **There will be countless opportunities for you to learn and grow.** Active participation in love relationships is a true first-hand experience of life. It gives us an opportunity to understand our human behavior in a way that feels real to us. There aren't any books (including this one) that can give you personal references that will be as vivid as your own for what you want to experience again or wish to avoid in the future.

🌱 **Special moments of love will be yours to enjoy and treasure forever.** As we grow older, the years pass by but the memories of special moments remain. It is the joy we experience in our special moments of love that are treasured for the rest of our lives. As most older people will verify, the experiences of love are the ones that are the most cherished.

🌱 **Your pride will swell from having made a difference in someone else's life.** Part of our love experience is the incredible feeling we get from helping another person find joy in their life. By being a dependable love partner, you can help your other half become a more empowered individual and a greater value to themselves and others.

☙ **The stability that love offers will comfort you in troubled times.** Many people find that the security of a committed love relationship is the base from which all of their success and happiness comes from. In our current troubling times, it's always a great comfort to have someone we love available for us to share our emotional burdens with.

☙ **Being loved by someone will bring you unique joy.** Most people feel that it's important to be respected by others. At the same time, it is also flattering to be told that you're an attractive and desirable person to the opposite sex. But these emotions pale in comparison to the joy of being loved and cherished by another human being.

In addition to the benefits listed above, you will receive the greatest gift of all by becoming a genuine loving person. This is a priceless quality that people dear to you will always like and admire about you. Authentic loving people are the only ones who we can really trust in our lives today.

DON'T PAY THE HIGH PRICE OF REGRET!

Unfortunately, the journey to love can involve painful experiences. Like a powerful punch in the stomach, real emotions like frustration, disappointment, sadness, and hurt are often experienced along the way causing us pain. But for most people, these emotions are temporary injuries to the ego and not permanent scars to the soul.

A big problem with emotional pain is that it will prevent some people from giving love a fair chance to succeed. In an effort to protect themselves from being hurt, many people will simply not give love their all. So while they succeed in avoiding short-term pain, they ruin their chances at gaining the higher value of long-term love.

In order to prevent this from happening, a wise individual must realize that the price of regret can be significantly higher than the price of short-term pain. Regret is like a terminal illness that starts slowly but gets progressively worse with age. Yet what we should have done in the past is of little value when it's too late to change the results. Regret may eventually take the form of chronic bitterness or deep-rooted cynicism. But perhaps worst of all, regret robs us of the peace of mind that we attain from knowing that we have given life and love our full effort.

SMART MOVE #21: SURRENDER YOUR EGO FOR LOVE

The final smart move to make in designing your love life is to surrender your ego in order for love to succeed. Don't let pride keep you from giving your love. Be willing to accept pain and disappointment over the short-term in order to receive the ever-lasting benefits of love over the long term.

What we want in our love lives is usually to have all the benefits of love with as little risk as possible. But such a pain-free approach to love is usually the very reason so many people never experience love in the first place. Investing too little of themselves, they predictably get little back.

I suggest that you seriously consider the following question for your own well-being:

What does God or my Higher Power want for me?

After careful examination, you might discover that your higher source wants you to become a more loving person. When love becomes your power source, then succeeding in relationships of any kind is almost always guaranteed.

THE FINAL BOTTOM LINE

You now have the power of specialized knowledge to guide your destiny to the love you desire. Commit to making only smart moves in your love life and let the odds of success weigh heavily in your favor.

In the game of love and in the bigger game of life, make sure that the final tally will show that you played with all of your being. Live your life to its fullest. Give yourself the complete freedom to love with the deep understanding that the only true failures in life are those people who never try or give up too easily.

My final observation is this:

Dating rocks when you rock!

After traveling all this way with me through this book, you can probably surmise that I believe that a woman who rocks is one whose thoughts and actions come from a kind heart and a mature mind.

Enjoy your amazing journey to love, treasure your most precious moments forever, and always remember to give love your all. If you do, then you'll be without a doubt an enlightened woman who truly rocks!

Good luck and God bless.

About the Author

Steve Nakamoto is a former human relations/communications instructor for Dale Carnegie & Associates and personal development trainer for world-renowned motivation and peak-performance expert Tony Robbins.

Steve has also spent several years as an international tour director taking clients on first-class vacation trips. With more than 200 cruises, Club Med vacations, Singles' Ski Weeks, and escorted vacation tours, the author has had a lot of first-hand experience learning about men and women of all ages, backgrounds, and cultures.

His first book, *Men Are Like Fish: What Every Woman Needs to Know about Catching a Man*, received Honorable Mention recognition in the *Writer's Digest 2000 Self-Published Non-Fiction Book Awards*. That book went on to sell foreign language translation rights to Spain, Japan, Israel, Thailand, Taiwan, Korea, Estonia, Russia, and the Czech Republic.

Steve has appeared on over 220 radio and television talk shows including NBC's *The Other Half* starring Dick Clark, Mario Lopez, Dorian Gregory, and Danny Bonaduce. He currently serves as the featured dating/relationship expert on iVillage.com's popular "Ask Mr. Answer Man" online discussion board where he offers an honest male perspective on day-to-day issues to women around the world.

For more information, visit www.DatingRocks.com.